LE
BIBLE STUD
BEH

Armageddon

Neil Wilson and Len Woods

MOODY PUBLISHERS

CHICAGO

Contents

For the latest information on other Left Behind series and Bible prophecy products, go to www.leftbehind.com. Sign up for a free e-mail update!

Foreword

Tim LaHaye and Jerry B. Jenkins

Jesus said, "Watch and wait" (Mark 13:32–37).

Even believers looking for the coming of Christ will be surprised at the Rapture. But it will be a delightful surprise—the fulfillment of our deepest longings. One of our goals in the Left Behind novels is to keep others from being surprised in the worst sense—by being caught off guard and left behind.

A large body of literature written in the last half century highlights the growing evidence that Christ's coming is quickly drawing near. We have written several books ourselves seeking to help people understand biblical passages about the end times. *Are We Living in the End Times?* (Tyndale), *The Tim LaHaye Prophecy Study Bible* (AMG), *Will I Be Left Behind?* (Tyndale), and *Perhaps Today* (Tyndale) all were written to help people understand biblical prophecy.

The Left Behind Bible study guide series from Moody Publishers uses material from the novels to illustrate an introduction to Bible prophecy. Authors Neil Wilson and Len Woods emphasize that the Left Behind stories are rooted in biblical themes. They bring together various prophetic passages of Scripture and plenty of thought-provoking questions, with the goal of getting you to live in the light of the imminent return of Christ.

These studies will help you discover what we wanted to show in the novels—that all the historical, technological, and theological pieces of the puzzle recorded in biblical prophecy are more plainly in place for Christ's return now than ever before. Technological advances commonplace today parallel scriptural pictures in such an uncanny way that they allow for prophesied events that even a generation ago seemed impossible.

Biblical prophecy doesn't look nearly as strange anymore. Our intent in the novels was to simply make the truth of the Bible come alive for fiction readers. That many people have been driven back to their Bibles is a wonderful outcome. In your hands is another vehicle that allows you to closely study the Bible texts that thrilled us and served as the basis for the fiction. We encourage you to become a wise student of God's Word and a watchful observer of the times.

Introduction

Neil Wilson and Len Woods

Welcome to this introductory study of end-times prophecy! We pray that you will find these studies helpful, challenging, and encouraging in your walk with Christ.

General interest in prophecy among Christians tends to behave very much like an active volcano. About once in each generation, seismic events in history grab everyone's attention, and the internal pressure to see events from God's point of view causes an eruption of prophetic concerns. Early in our generation toward the end of the 1960s, we experienced just such an eruption with the turbulence surrounding the Vietnam conflict, the heating up of the Cold War, the rise of the Jesus Movement, and the publication of Hal Lindsay's book *The Late Great Planet Earth,* among other things. Larry Norman's song "I Wish We'd All Been Ready" struck a chord of longing and urged our generation to get serious about Jesus. He was coming like a thief in the night. Prophetic students pointed to the rebirth of the nation of Israel and the rapidly closing time period following that event as an indisputable clue to Christ's coming. We tried to get ready—for a while.

Unfortunately, like many examples of public fascination, the wide interest in prophetic issues gradually dwindled to the faithful remnant, who continually read the signs of the times and served the body of Christ with urgent warnings. The volcano seemed to go silent. Here and there, prophecy conferences still gathered. Books were written, papers presented, and even heated arguments raged behind closed doors. The world quickly went on its way to more hopeful outlooks: the fall of the Berlin Wall, the explosive rise of the stock market, and mur-mured promises that the world might finally be headed toward life as a kinder, gentler place. Continual background trouble was ignored. Even the body of Christ seemed fascinated with herself. The potential of church growth achieved by appealing to seekers and making it very easy to slide into the church created an atmosphere where judgment and Christ's second com-ing sounded a little harsh and unfriendly. The church became, in many ways, too successful to long for rapture. The distant rumble of the volcano was drowned out by the music of worship that too often sounded a lot more like entertainment than serious consideration of the majesty of God.

The arrival of new centuries and the much rarer dawn of new millenniums have usually created a suspicion that more than just a calendar time line might be coming to an end. Recently, terms like Y2K became shorthand for fearful brooding over the sudden realization that our entire civilization seemed dependent on countless computers remaining sane in spite of a simple change in their internal clocks. Many expected a cyber meltdown. Some predicted a new Dark Ages. Thousands stockpiled food, water, and guns. And most of us wondered what would happen. Christians who knew prophecy simply couldn't see cataclysmic Y2K scenarios indicated in the Bible. Their more or less confident counsel to trust in God's sovereignty was often met with suspicion and derision by those practical believers, whose motto seemed to be "God helps those who help themselves." Y2K caught the church unprepared.

In the predawn jitters of the new millennium, a book was published that seemed to almost instantly grab the imagination of millions. *Left Behind* became plausible fiction. As Tim LaHaye and Jerry Jenkins have repeatedly stated, one of their primary goals was to demonstrate that all the technology was already in place to allow prophetic events to occur that previous generations had found inconceivable. A volcano of interest in prophecy began to rumble. The tremors found their way to the shelves of the largest general market bookstores as millions of the *Left Behind* books left the stores. Many Christians reported surprise over their own lack of understanding of what seems so apparent throughout Scripture. In the years that have followed the publication of the first novel, there has been a healthy movement toward greater acknowledgment that God has a plan for this world, and a deadline is approaching. His Word makes that fact clear, and the events of history are providing confirming echoes.

We trust these studies will tune your heart and mind to the purposes of God. We hope that as a result of studying his Word you will long for your daily life to harmonize with God's purposes. We pray that you increasingly will be intent on doing what God has set before you, glancing from time to time at the horizon, anticipating your personal encounter with the Lord! May your prayers frequently include, "Maranatha!"—Lord, come quickly!

How to Get the Most from Your Study

Depending on your background and experiences, the Left Behind studies will

- Help you begin to answer some important questions that may have occurred to you as you were reading the Left Behind novels,

- Introduce you to the serious study of biblical prophecy,

- Provide you with a starting point for a personal review of biblical prophecy that you remember hearing about as you were growing up, or

- Offer you a format to use in meeting with others to discuss not only the Left Behind novels but also the Bible texts that inspired the stories.

If you are using these studies on your own, you will establish your own pace. A thoughtful consideration of the Bible passages, questions, and quotes from the Left Behind series and other books will require a minimum of an hour for each lesson.

If you will be discussing these lessons as part of a group, make sure you review each lesson on your own. Your efforts in preparation will result in a number of personal benefits:

- You will have thought through some of the most important questions and be less prone to "shallow answers."

- You will have a good sense of the direction of the discussion.

- You will have an opportunity to do some added research if you discover an area or question that you know will be beyond the scope of the group discussion.

- Since a group will probably not be able to cover every question in each lesson because of time constraints, your preparation will allow you to fill in the gaps.

Tools to Use

- Make sure you have a Bible you can read easily.

- Most of the quotes in these studies come from the New Living Translation. If your Bible is a different version, get in the habit of comparing the verses.

- Consider reading some of the excellent books available today for the study of prophecy. You will find helpful suggestions in the endnotes.

- Put some mileage on your pen or pencil. Take time to write out answers to the questions as you prepare each lesson.

- Continually place your life before God. Ultimately, your study of prophecy ought to deepen your awareness of both his sovereignty and compassion. You will appreciate the overwhelming aspects of God's love, mercy, and grace toward you even more as you get a wider view of his grandeur and glory.

Leading a Group Through the Left Behind Studies

Leading a Bible study on prophecy can be daunting to any teacher. When it comes to prophecy, all of us are students; we've all got a lot to learn. Approaching this study as a fresh opportunity to ask questions, to seek the Lord and his Word for answers, and to help others in the process will take the burden of being "the teacher" off your shoulders.

Remember that it's helpful to be confident in what you know as long as you're not confident you know everything. The study of prophecy does bring up many questions for which the most honest answer is, "We don't know." God has, however, given us more information in his Word than he is often given credit for. To use the apostle Paul's language, we may see some things sharply and other things dimly, but that's so much better than being in the dark. Take a careful look at Tim LaHaye's article "How to Study Prophecy," and encourage your group to read it. It provides valuable guidelines as you prepare for these discussions.

No matter the level of knowledge you or your group may have, set your sights on increasing your group's interest in the study of prophecy as well as deepening their commitment to living for Christ. Keep your group focused on the need to know Jesus better. Ultimately, it's hard to get excited about expecting a stranger. The more intimately we get to know Jesus, the more we long to see him. Consider using as a motto for your group the words of Paul, "Yet I am not ashamed, because I know whom I have believed, and am convinced that he is able to guard what I have entrusted to him for that day" (2 Timothy 1:12 NIV).

Prophecy and evangelism travel together. A study like this can provide unexpected opportunities to share the gospel. We tend to think that evangelistic conversations are primarily a backward look with a present application—God has accomplished certain gracious things through Christ and his death and resurrection; therefore, what shall we do today? Prophecy reverses the discussion, creating a forward look with a present application—God promises he will do these things tomorrow; therefore, how shall we live today? Be prayerfully alert to opportunities during and after studies to interact seriously with group members about the state of their souls. Tim LaHaye and Jerry Jenkins have letters from hundreds of readers of the Left Behind series who came to faith in Christ in part as a result of their exposure to prophecy. Pray that God will use your study to accomplish his purposes in others' lives, including yours.

Several Helpful Tools

Bibles: Encourage group members to bring and use their Bibles. We've quoted in the workbook the verses being discussed in each lesson, but having the full context of the verses available to examine is often helpful. We recommend that you have on hand for consultation at least one copy of a trustworthy study Bible that highlights prophetic issues, such as the *Ryrie Study Bible* (Moody Press) or the *Tim LaHaye Prophecy Study Bible* (AMG Publishers).

Bible Concordance and Bible Dictionary: Each of these tools can assist a group in the process of finding specific passages in Scripture or gaining a perspective on a particular biblical theme or word.

Resource Books: The endnotes for each lesson include a number of books from which insightful quotes have been drawn. If members in your group have access to these books, encourage them to make the volumes available for others to read.

Left Behind Novels: Because there are several editions of the books, you may discover some discrepancies in the page listings of the quotes from the novels and the particular books you have. A little search of the pages nearby will usually get you to the right place.

Hints for Group Sessions

1. Encourage participants to review and prepare as much of each lesson as they are able in advance. Remind them it will help the learning process if they have been thinking about the issues and subjects before the session.
2. As you prepare the lessons, decide what questions you will make your focus for discussion. Unless your time is open-ended and your group highly motivated, you will not be able to cover every question adequately in an hour.
3. Only experience with your particular group will give you a sense of how much ground you can cover each session.
4. Consider appointing different group members to ask the questions. That will take the spotlight off you and allow them to participate in a comfortable way.
5. Take time in each session for feedback and questions from the group. These spontaneous reflections will give you a good sense of how much the group is learning, integrating, and being affected by the lessons.

The Place of Prayer

Make it a point to pray with the group and for the group during the study. Use part of your preparation time to bring each person from the group before God in prayer. Open and close each session by asking God, who alone knows the full meaning of every prophecy he has inspired in his Word, to open your hearts and minds to understand and respond in practical, wholehearted ways to the truth of Scripture.

How to Study Bible Prophecy

Tim LaHaye

Prophecy is God's road map to show us where history is going. The Bible's predictions claim literal and specific fulfillments that verify that such prophecies are indeed from God. The key to interpreting Bible prophecy is in discerning what is literal and what is symbolic. Therefore, the best way to avoid confusion in the study of prophetic Scripture is to follow these simple directions:

1. Interpret prophecy literally wherever possible. God meant what he said and said what he meant when he inspired "holy men of God [who] spake as they were moved by the Holy Ghost" (2 Peter 1:21 KJV) to write the Bible. Consequently we can take the Bible literally most of the time. Where God intends for us to interpret symbolically he also makes it obvious. One of the reasons the book of Revelation is difficult for some people to understand is that they try to spiritualize the symbols used in the book. However, since many Old Testament prophecies have already been literally fulfilled, such as God turning water to blood (Exodus 4:9; 7:17–21), it should not be difficult to imagine that future prophetic events can and will be literally fulfilled at the appropriate time. Only when symbols or figures of speech make absolutely no literal sense should anything but a literal interpretation be sought.

2. Prophecies concerning Israel and the church should not be transposed. The promises of God to Israel to be fulfilled "in the latter days," particularly those concerning Israel's punishment during the Tribulation, have absolutely nothing to do with the church. The Bible gives specific promises for the church that she will be raptured into heaven before the Tribulation (John 14:2–3; 1 Corinthians 15:51–52; 1 Thessalonians 4:13–18).

3. For symbolic passages, compare Scripture with Scripture. The Bible is not contradictory. Even though written by numerous divinely inspired men over a period of sixteen hundred years, it is supernaturally consistent in its use of terms. For example, the word "beast" is used thirty-four times in Revelation and many other times in Scripture. Daniel explains that the word is symbolic of either a king or kingdom (see Daniel 7–8). By examining the contexts in Revelation and Daniel, you will find that "beast" has the same meaning in both books. Many other symbols used in Revelation are also taken directly from the Old Testament. These include "the tree of life" (Revelation 2:7; 22:2, 14), "the Book of Life" (Revelation 3:5), and Babylon (Revelation 14:8ff.).

Some symbols in Revelation are drawn from other New Testament passages. These include terms such as "the word of God" (1:2, 9ff.), "Son of Man" (1:13; 14:14), "marriage supper" (19:9), "the bride" (21:9; 22:17), "first resurrection" (20:5–6), and "second death" (2:11;

20:6, 14; 21:8). Other symbols in Revelation are explained and identified in their context. For example, "Alpha and Omega" represents Jesus Christ (1:8; 21:6; 22:13); the "seven candlesticks" (1:13, 20) are the seven churches; the "dragon" is Satan (12:3ff.); and the "man child" is Jesus (12:5, 13).

Though some prophetic passages should be interpreted symbolically, it is important to remember that symbols in the Bible depict real people, things, and events. For example, the "seven candlesticks" in Revelation 1 represent real churches that actually existed when the prophecy was given.

Keeping the three points above in mind will provide you with a confident approach to prophetic Scriptures and guard against a multitude of errors. Allow God's Word always to be your final guide.

(Adapted from the *Tim LaHaye Prophecy Study Bible,* AMG Publishers, used with permission.)

Overview of the End Times

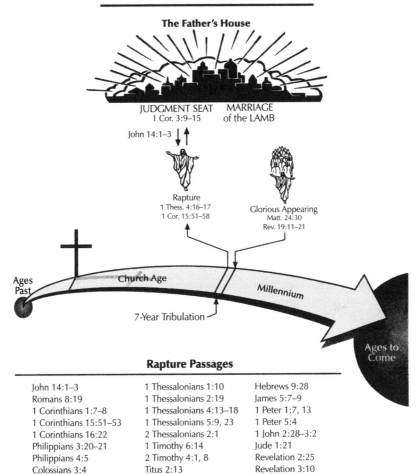

End-Times Overview
Matthew 24:29–31

The Father's House

JUDGMENT SEAT
1 Cor. 3:9–15

MARRIAGE
of the LAMB

John 14:1–3

Rapture
1 Thess. 4:16–17
1 Cor. 15:51–58

Glorious Appearing
Matt. 24:30
Rev. 19:11–21

Ages
Past

Church Age

Millennium

7-Year Tribulation

Ages to
Come

Rapture Passages

John 14:1–3	1 Thessalonians 1:10	Hebrews 9:28
Romans 8:19	1 Thessalonians 2:19	James 5:7–9
1 Corinthians 1:7–8	1 Thessalonians 4:13–18	1 Peter 1:7, 13
1 Corinthians 15:51–53	1 Thessalonians 5:9, 23	1 Peter 5:4
1 Corinthians 16:22	2 Thessalonians 2:1	1 John 2:28–3:2
Philippians 3:20–21	1 Timothy 6:14	Jude 1:21
Philippians 4:5	2 Timothy 4:1, 8	Revelation 2:25
Colossians 3:4	Titus 2:13	Revelation 3:10

Second Coming Passages

Daniel 2:44–45	Mark 13:14–27	1 Peter 4:12–13
Daniel 7:9–14	Mark 14:62	2 Peter 3:1–14
Daniel 12:1–3	Luke 21:25–28	Jude 1:14–15
Zechariah 12:10	Acts 1:9–11	Revelation 1:7
Zechariah 14:1–15	Acts 3:19–21	Revelation 19:11–20:6
Matthew 13:41	1 Thessalonians 3:13	Revelation 22:7, 12, 20
Matthew 24:15–31	2 Thessalonians 1:6–10	
Matthew 26:64	2 Thessalonians 2:8	

LEFT

BEHIND

Armageddon

Lesson 1
To End All Wars

1. What do you think of when you hear the word *Armageddon?*

_____

_____

_____

_____

2. How do people typically use the word *Armageddon?*

_____

_____

_____

_____

> "The word *Armageddon* has Hebrew roots, with the word *Har* meaning 'mountain' or 'hill,' and *Magedon* being a reference to the ruins of an ancient city that overlooks the Valley of Esdraelon in northern Israel." [1]
>
> Tim LaHaye and Thomas Ice

3. In your opinion, what are the odds there will be a World War III or some large-scale conflict involving weapons of mass destruction in the next ten years? Why?

_____

_____

_____

The Horrors of War

In all of human history there have been only a few recorded years of world peace. War has been the rule rather than the exception. Below are some of the more famous statements about war. And remember—Armageddon will be far worse than any war ever seen on earth.

"There is many a boy here today who looks on war as all glory; but boys, it is all hell. You can bear this warning voice to generations yet to come. I look upon war with horror."

William Tecumseh Sherman, U.S. general,
from a speech, August 1880

"All wars are popular for the first thirty days."

Attributed to Arthur Schlesinger Jr., U.S. historian

"The guerrilla fights the war of the flea, and his military enemy suffers the dog's disadvantages: too much to defend; too small, ubiquitous, and agile an enemy to come to grips with."

Robert Taber, U.S. writer,
from *War of the Flea* (1965)

"A war regarded as inevitable or even probable, and therefore much prepared for, has a very good chance of being fought."

George F. Kennan, U.S. diplomat and scholar,
from *The Cloud of Danger* (1977)

"You no more win a war than you can win an earthquake."

Jeannette Rankin, U.S. legislator

"Do not let us speak of darker days; let us rather speak of sterner days. These are not dark days: these are great days—the greatest days our country has ever lived."

Winston Churchill, British prime minister,
from a speech, October 29, 1941

"It is well that war is so terrible; else we would grow too fond of it."

Robert E. Lee, U.S. general, to another general
during the Battle of Fredericksburg (1862)

Unfolding the Story

(*Armageddon*, pp. 332–34)

The eleventh book in the best-selling Left Behind series is titled *Armageddon*. It deals with the events prophesied in the Bible that will lead up to the climactic battle of the ages.

In the following scene, the Jewish evangelist Tsion Ben-Judah tells a crowd in Jerusalem how unfolding events fulfill the ancient prophecies of both Old and New Testaments:

AS WORD SPREAD that Tsion Ben-Judah was at the Wailing Wall preaching to the Jews, more and more streamed in.

"These Scriptures foretell what is going to happen soon!" he said. "Listen to the words of Peter: 'The day of the Lord will come as a thief in the night, in which the heavens will pass away with a great noise, and the elements will melt with fervent heat; both the earth and the works that are in it will be burned up. Therefore, since all these things will be dissolved, what manner of persons ought you to be in holy conduct and godliness, looking for and hastening the coming of the day of God, because of which the heavens will be dissolved, being on fire, and the elements will melt with fervent heat? Nevertheless we, according to His promise, look for new heavens and a new earth in which righteousness dwells.'

"That is our promise, what we have been looking for! For how many generations have we prayed for peace? Soon, after the conflict, eternal peace!

"Messiah will return as King of kings. He promised to return, to conquer Satan, and to set up his millennial kingdom, reestablishing Israel and making Jerusalem the capital forever!

"With probably a billion of Messiah's followers already removed from this earth, and with the disappearances of seven years ago that were predicted more than two thousand years before, many Jews and Gentiles have turned to Jesus Christ as the true Messiah.

"Our own prophet Joel foretold of these very days. Listen to the words of Holy Scripture: 'It shall come to pass afterward that I will pour out My Spirit on all flesh; your sons and your daughters shall prophesy, your old men shall dream dreams, your young men shall see visions. And also on My menservants and on My maidservants I will pour out My Spirit in those days.

'And I will show wonders in the heavens and in the earth: blood and fire and pillars of smoke. The sun shall be turned into darkness, and the moon into blood, before the coming of the great and awesome day of the Lord. And it shall come to pass that whoever calls on the name of the Lord shall be saved. For in Mount Zion and in Jerusalem there shall be deliverance, as the Lord has said, among the remnant whom the Lord calls.'

"You are that remnant, people of Israel. Turn to Messiah today! Listen further to the prophecy of Joel and see if it does not reflect these very days! 'For behold, in those days and at that time, when I bring back the captives of Judah and Jerusalem, I will also gather all nations, and bring them down to the Valley of Jehoshaphat; and I will enter into judgment with them there on account of My people, My heritage Israel.'"

4. Was Tsion's message good news or bad news? Why?

_____

_____

_____

_____

_____

5. What kind of future do the Scriptures cited by Tsion foretell for planet Earth? For Israel?

_____

_____

_____

_____

_____

_____

6. The prophet Joel, quoted by Tsion, credits whom for bringing all the nations of the earth against Israel?

_____

_____

_____

_____

"The most important benefit from studying prophecy is the challenge to live in light of our ultimate destiny. God has given us adequate revelation concerning the future, though many questions remain. We can trust God with the unknown, and we need to believe and respond to the truth he has given us concerning the life to come. Prophecy by its very nature reveals a sovereign God who is omniscient, who knows the future as well as the past, and who is able to give us guidance and direction as we seek to live for him. Biblical prophecy, then, gives hope for the future as well as comfort and zeal for the present." [2]

John Walvoord

Back to Reality

Think about current events and unfolding trends in our world today: religious confusion, a global economy (so interconnected that if Wall Street "hiccups," the whole world is affected), the political and cultural volatility in many regions, rogue nations and terrorist groups eager to get their hands on weapons of mass destruction, natural disasters, an overt and growing anti-Semitism, the increasing number of countries that are willing to surrender their sovereignty to the United Nations. These are just a few of the troubling issues facing the world.

7. Besides the trends listed above, what other possible signs of the end times do you see on the horizon?

_____

_____

_____

_____

_____

8. Why do you think so many people believe that humanity can fix its problems without help from above?

_____

_____

_____

_____

9. How much faith do you have in the world's most powerful nations or in organizations like the United Nations to maintain peace on earth? Why?

_____

_____

_____

_____

If you haven't done so recently, review the chart in the front pages of this workbook that gives an overview of end-times events leading up to Armageddon.

> "Since God never leaves anything undone or half-finished, we can be sure that he will not leave any loose ends in bringing the Great Tribulation to a close. In fact, this period during which Satan has been in command and evil has run rampant will end with the devil's most foolish move of all. It's an all-out attempt to use his evil forces to defeat Jesus Christ and the armies of heaven in head-on combat." [3]
>
> Tony Evans

Understanding the Word

To properly understand the cataclysmic finale for planet Earth, the terrible battle the Bible calls Armageddon, we need to have a grasp of the events leading up to it. Previous study guides in this series have focused on the Rapture, the Antichrist, and the judgments of the Tribulation. In this lesson, our focus is on the inevitability of a final showdown between the mastermind of evil, Satan himself, and almighty God.

When we strip away all the details, there stands our sovereign Creator, who is moving all events toward their appointed conclusion, and Satan, the one who hates God and seeks to thwart his plans and ruin his people. Revelation 12:1–17 shows us graphically the devilish hatred that will culminate in Armageddon:

> *Then I witnessed in heaven an event of great significance. I saw a woman clothed with the sun, with the moon beneath her feet, and a crown of twelve stars on her head. She was pregnant, and she cried out in the pain of labor as she awaited her delivery.*

Suddenly, I witnessed in heaven another significant event. I saw a large red dragon with seven heads and ten horns, with seven crowns on his heads. His tail dragged down one-third of the stars, which he threw to the earth. He stood before the woman as she was about to give birth to her child, ready to devour the baby as soon as it was born.

She gave birth to a boy who was to rule all nations with an iron rod. And the child was snatched away from the dragon and was caught up to God and to his throne. And the woman fled into the wilderness, where God had prepared a place to give her care for 1,260 days.

Then there was war in heaven. Michael and the angels under his command fought the dragon and his angels. And the dragon lost the battle and was forced out of heaven. This great dragon—the ancient serpent called the Devil, or Satan, the one deceiving the whole world—was thrown down to the earth with all his angels.

Then I heard a loud voice shouting across the heavens,

"It has happened at last—the salvation and power and kingdom of our God, and the authority of his Christ! For the Accuser has been thrown down to earth—the one who accused our brothers and sisters before our God day and night. And they have defeated him because of the blood of the Lamb and because of their testimony. And they were not afraid to die. Rejoice, O heavens! And you who live in the heavens, rejoice! But terror will come on the earth and the sea. For the Devil has come down to you in great anger, and he knows that he has little time."

And when the dragon realized that he had been thrown down to the earth, he pursued the woman who had given birth to the child. But she was given two wings like those of a great eagle. This allowed her to fly to a place prepared for her in the wilderness, where she would be cared for and protected from the dragon for a time, times, and half a time.

Then the dragon tried to drown the woman with a flood of water that flowed from its mouth. But the earth helped her by opening its mouth and swallowing the river that gushed out from the mouth of the dragon. Then the dragon became angry at the woman, and he declared war against the rest of her children—all who keep God's commandments and confess that they belong to Jesus.

10. The woman in Revelation 12 represents Israel; the dragon represents Satan. What does this passage reveal about Satan's "feelings" toward Israel? How is he described?

_____

_____

_____

11. Notice that while the devil hates and battles against God, neither the Father nor the Son enter the battle directly. The Creator doesn't fight the creature. God has a powerful part of creation that battles the devil. How are God's armies described? What is the outcome?

_____

_____

_____

"The key to Armageddon is Satan's attempt to defeat God by destroying Israel (Revelation 12:13–17). . . . Even though Satan knows it is futile to wage war against God because the outcome was decided at the Cross, he believes that if he could eradicate Israel, he would destroy God's covenant promises. That would make God a liar. . . .

Satan can't get at God directly, so he will go after God's people. That's why he wants Israel, and that's why Israel will never know real peace until Jesus Christ sits on the throne of David. The devil will always keep some nation or group stirred up to come at Israel from other directions." [4]

Tony Evans

It's essential to remember that though Satan hates God and the things of God, he is not calling the shots in the unfolding of future events. Yes, he wants to gather the nations at Armageddon to wreak maximum havoc and destruction, but he is also playing right into God's hands. Consider this passage from Zechariah 12:1–14:

This message concerning the fate of Israel came from the LORD: "This message is from the LORD, who stretched out the heavens, laid the foundations of the earth, and formed the spirit within humans. I will make Jerusalem and Judah like an intoxicating drink to all the nearby nations that send their armies to besiege Jerusalem. On that day I will make Jerusalem a heavy stone, a burden for the world. None of the nations who try to lift it will escape unscathed.

"On that day, says the LORD, I will cause every horse to panic and every rider to lose his nerve. I will watch over the people of Judah, but I will blind the horses of her enemies. And the clans of Judah will say to themselves, 'The people of Jerusalem have found strength in the LORD Almighty, their God.'

"On that day I will make the clans of Judah like a brazier that sets a woodpile ablaze or like a burning torch among sheaves of grain. They will burn up all the neighboring nations right and left, while the people living in Jerusalem remain secure. The LORD will *give victory to the rest of Judah first, before Jerusalem, so that the people of Jerusalem and the royal line of David will not have greater honor than the rest of Judah. On that day the Lord will defend the people of Jerusalem; the weakest among them will be as mighty as King David! And the royal descendants will be like God, like the angel of the Lord who goes before them! For my plan is to destroy all the nations that come against Jerusalem.*

"Then I will pour out a spirit of grace and prayer on the family of David and on all the people of Jerusalem. They will look on me whom they have pierced and mourn for him as for an only son. They will grieve bitterly for him as for a firstborn son who has died. The sorrow and mourning in Jerusalem on that day will be like the grievous mourning of Hadad-rimmon in the valley of Megiddo.

"All Israel will weep in profound sorrow, each family by itself, with the husbands and wives in separate groups. The family of David will mourn, along with the family of Nathan, the family of Levi, and the family of Shimei. Each of the surviving families from Judah will mourn separately, husbands and wives apart."

12. Who is the primary actor and director in this passage? Who is orchestrating these events?

_____

_____

_____

13. What does this passage suggest about God's plan and intentions at Armageddon?

_____

_____

_____

"Armageddon will be the last great war of history, and it will take place in Israel in conjunction with the second coming of Christ. . . . The site where this will occur is the plain of Esdraelon, around the hill of Megiddo, in northern Israel about twenty miles south-southeast of Haifa. . . . According to the Bible, great armies from the east and the west will gather and assemble on this plain. There will be threats to the power of the Antichrist from the south, and he will move to destroy a revived Babylon in the east before finally turning his forces toward Jerusalem to subdue and destroy it. As he and his armies approach Jerusalem, God will intervene and Jesus Christ will return to rescue his people Israel. The Lord and his angelic army will destroy the armies, capture the Antichrist and the False Prophet, and cast them into the Lake of Fire (Revelation 19:11–21)." [5]

Tim LaHaye and Thomas Ice

Finding the Connection

(*Armageddon*, pp. 219–22)

In book eleven of the Left Behind series, Chloe Williams, one of the original members of the Tribulation Force, is captured by the forces of Antichrist, given truth serum, and interrogated.

These scenes between Chloe and Jock accurately depict (on both the interpersonal and intrapersonal levels) the age-old battle between good and evil, and the ultimate victory of good:

> **JOCK STOOD AND LOOKED** out the door, breathing heavily. Presently he moved to Chloe's chair and removed the surgical tubing and receptacle. He unstrapped her.
>
> "We're finished?" she said.
>
> "No, but you have ingested the maximum dose. I've never seen anything like it. We can sit and chat for a few minutes, and if that last hit kicks in and makes you come to your senses, you let me know."
>
> "Let's talk about you, Jock. What got you so fired up about Carpathia?"
>
> "Oh no, we're not going there. You can just leave me alone. You obviously believe what you believe. That's impressive, I'll give you that. Misguided, but impressive. That's the problem with religious extremists."
>
> "Oh, that's what we are?" she said.
>
> "Of course."
>
> "You'd like to lump us with people who kill in the name of their faith, wouldn't you?"
>
> "You're as extreme as they come, ma'am."
>
> "We don't kill people who don't agree with us. We don't erect statues of our God everywhere and require by law that everyone bow and scrape before them three times a day. We offer the truth, show people the way, call them to God. But we don't force them."
>
> Jock sat heavily. "Do you realize you're going to die tomorrow?"
>
> "I had an inkling."
>
> "And that doesn't bother you?"
>
> "Of course it does. I'm scared."
>
> "And you're never going to see your husband, your baby, your loved ones and friends again."
>
> "If I thought that was true, that would be a different story."

"I get it. Pie in the sky by-and-by. You're all going to be floating around on clouds someday—playing your harps and wearing white robes."

"I hope you're right about the pie but not the harps.". . .

She plunged on. "Jock, do you realize that the day is coming—and much sooner than you think—when everyone will have to acknowledge God and his Son?"

"Think so?"

"It is written: 'As I live,' says the Lord, 'every knee shall bow to Me, and every tongue shall confess to God.'"

"Well, honey, not me."

"Sorry, Jock. 'Each of us shall give account of himself to God.'"

"My god is Carpathia. That's good enough for me."

"What about when Jesus wins?"

"He wins?"

"'Therefore God also has highly exalted Him and given Him the name which is above every name, that at the name of Jesus every knee should bow, of those in heaven, and of those on earth, and of those under the earth, and that every tongue should confess that Jesus Christ is Lord, to the glory of God the Father.'"

"I hope all that gives you some comfort when you're standing in the hot sun tomorrow morning, smelling that smell, seeing heads roll, and knowing yours will be next. Maybe I'm not the interrogator I thought I was, and maybe you paid a lot of money to be trained and prepped for truth serum. But there's nothing that brings clarity to the mind like knowing you're next in the guillotine line.

"I'll be watching you in the morning, girl. My money says you'll be shaking and wailing and pleading for one more chance to save yourself."

14. Choe speaks of everyone giving an "account of himself to God." In what sense are *you* ready for this ultimate "audit"? How about your friends and loved ones?

_____

_____

_____

_____

_____

_____

15. If Chloe is so certain that "Jesus wins" and so convinced that she *will* see her loved ones in the life to come, why is she still scared? Does the prospect of dying unnerve or frighten you? Why or why not?

_____

_____

_____

_____

_____

_____

16. Chloe quotes Philippians 2:9–11, a passage that reveals the ultimate exaltation of Christ. Jock responds sarcastically, "I hope that gives you some comfort." What do *you* find comforting about the assurance that Jesus is Lord over all, and that one day all creatures will acknowledge this fact?

_____

_____

_____

_____

_____

_____

Making the Change

17. How would you describe the bitterness of Satan behind the biblical events like Matthew 2:13–18 (Herod's slaughter of the innocents)? To what degree do you see that same hatred behind recent events, such as the Holocaust?

_____

_____

_____

_____

_____

18. In what ways have you experienced Satan's hatred against you? How does he try to keep you from drawing near to God and from doing the will of God?

_____

_____

_____

_____

_____

19. How does it affect you to know that your soul has a sworn enemy who hates you and would like to destroy you (see 1 Peter 5:8)? What needs to change in your life to keep you from being devoured by the Evil One?

_____

_____

_____

_____

_____

_____

> "Even when Satan is doing his stuff, he is actually accomplishing God's program. The devil is a puppet on God's string. On Satan's best day, he is helping achieve the program of God. Don't ever forget that." [6]
>
> Tony Evans

Pursuing the Truth

(*Ephesians* 6:11–13 tells us:)

> *Put on all of God's armor so that you will be able to stand firm against all strategies and tricks of the Devil. For we are not fighting against people made of flesh and blood, but against the evil rulers and authorities of the unseen world, against those mighty powers of darkness who rule this world, and against wicked spirits in the heavenly realms. Use every piece of God's armor to resist the enemy in the time of evil, so that after the battle you will still be standing firm.*

20. What does this passage say about our world's prospects for global peace? Do we live in peacetime, or in a time of cosmic war?

_____

_____

_____

_____

21. What are some of the devil's most effective strategies and tricks in *your* life?

_____

_____

_____

_____

_____

22. James 4:7 says, "Humble yourselves before God. Resist the Devil, and he will flee from you." Are we to be passive or active in relating to the devil? What does that look like in everyday terms? In what areas are you resisting Satan's attacks today?

_____

_____

_____

_____

_____

_____

Lesson in Review . . .

- The Battle of Armageddon will be the grand finale of the cosmic war that has been raging since before time.
- Satan will conspire to draw the nations of the world to the plain of Megiddo in northern Israel in a last-ditch effort to destroy the people of God.
- This devilish strategy is right in line with God's eternal purposes. He is sovereign and will once again demonstrate his infinite power and ultimate authority over the Evil One.

LEFT

BEHIND

Armageddon

Lesson 2
The Gathering Storm

1. To what evidence or events would you point to convince a skeptical friend that perhaps this world (as we know it) really *is* drawing to a close?

   _____

   _____

   _____

   _____

   _____

2. In contrast, what ideas or evidence have you heard skeptics use to state their assumption that the world will simply go on indefinitely?

   _____

   _____

   _____

   _____

Unfolding the Story
(*Armageddon*, pp. 334–36)

One of the central characters in the Left Behind novels is Tsion Ben-Judah, a former rabbinical scholar and Israeli statesman. After studying the biblical prophecies about Messiah, Tsion became a follower of Jesus Christ and revealed his faith on international television. In the novels, while eluding the forces of Antichrist, Tsion has used the Internet to teach the truth of Christ to more than a billion people daily.

In the scene below, on the verge of Armageddon and the second coming of Christ, Tsion has traveled to Jerusalem to seek more converts:

BUCK WAS ANSWERING QUESTIONS, praying with people, and all the while trying to listen to Tsion, who seemed to have found a second wind.

"The Day of the Lord is upon us," he said. "And lest there be any among you who still doubt, let me tell you what the prophecies say will happen after the armies of the world have gathered at Armageddon—which, as we all know, they are now doing. . . . They are rallying now, planning our destruction.

"And yet the Scriptures say that when they have gathered there, it will be time for the seventh angel to pour out his bowl into the air. Do you know what this refers to, men of Israel? The drying of the Euphrates was the sixth Bowl Judgment of God on the earth, the twentieth of his judgments since the Rapture.

"The seventh Bowl Judgment shall be the last, and do you know what it entails? When this bowl has been poured out, the Bible says 'a loud voice came out of the temple of heaven, from the throne saying, "It is done!"' How like the pronouncement of the spotless Lamb of God on the cross when he cried out, 'It is finished.'

"'And there were noises and thunderings and lightnings; and there was a great earthquake, such a mighty and great earthquake as had not occurred since men were on the earth.'

"Let me warn you, my countrymen. This earthquake will cover the entire world. Think of it! The Bible says that 'every island fled away, and the mountains were not found.' The mountains were not found! The elevation of the entire globe will be sea level! Who can survive such a catastrophe?

"The prophecy goes on to say that 'great hail from heaven fell upon men, each hailstone about the weight of a talent.' Beloved, a talent weighs between seventy-five and one hundred pounds! Who has ever heard of such hailstones? They will crush men and women to death! And the Scriptures say men will blaspheme God because of the plague of the hail, 'since that plague was exceedingly great.' Well, I should say it will be! Turn and repent now! Be counted among the army of God, not that of his enemy.

"Do you know what will happen here, right here in Jerusalem? It will be the only city in the world spared the devastating destruction of the greatest earthquake ever known to man. The Bible says, 'Now the great city'—that's Jerusalem—'was divided into three parts, and the cities of the nations fell.'

"That, my brothers, is good news. Jerusalem will be made more beautiful, more efficient. It will be prepared for its role as the new capital in Messiah's thousand-year kingdom. . . . How will we know when this is about to come to pass? It will be preceded by the destruction of Babylon. Yes, the destruction of Babylon!"

3. According to Tsion's message, based on the book of Revelation, what are the final seventh Bowl Judgments? How do they relate to Armageddon?

_____

_____

_____

_____

_____

_____

4. What natural (or supernatural) disasters will come just before the second coming of Christ, according to Tsion's teaching?

_____

_____

_____

_____

_____

5. What will happen to Jerusalem? to Babylon?

_____

_____

_____

_____

_____

Back to Reality

Perhaps as you have read the Left Behind novels and worked through these study guides, you have been both amazed at the rapid-fire unfolding of events and confused about their order.

There is much debate, even among conservative scholars, about the sequence of events. As the storm gathers, many of the divine judgments and human activities during earth's final days seem bunched together.

6. While events like the destruction of Saddam Hussein's regime are still unfolding in the Middle East, in what ways have you become more aware of the details of that region and its relation to the land of Israel?

_____

_____

_____

_____

_____

_____

7. As we've learned, the war to end all wars will take place inside the borders of and will target Israel. The nations of the world will gather in an attempt to obliterate the Jewish people and state. What specific signs of growing anti-Semitism in the news would indicate to you that the pieces of the end-times puzzle seem to be taking shape even today?

_____

_____

_____

_____

_____

_____

8. It is amazing how popular some so-called psychics are (so often impossibly vague or dead wrong in their predictions!). Their whimsical and contradictory "prophecies" get updated weekly on the covers of supermarket tabloids. Why do you think so many people disregard

the Bible's foretelling of the future—especially when it has been 100 percent accurate on countless other prophecies?

_____

_____

_____

_____

_____

_____

Understanding the Word

As we've seen in the previous Left Behind study guides, the Bible reveals many details about end-time characters, places, and events. Armageddon is both a place and an event. Scripture gives us some specific indications about what will transpire in the days and moments leading up to this climactic battle. One significant event that will pave the way for Armageddon is the sixth Bowl Judgment:

> *Then the sixth angel poured out his bowl on the great Euphrates River, and it dried up so that the kings from the east could march their armies westward without hindrance. And I saw three evil spirits that looked like frogs leap from the mouth of the dragon, the beast, and the false prophet. These miracle-working demons caused all the rulers of the world to gather for battle against the Lord on that great judgment day of God Almighty.*
>
> *"Take note: I will come as unexpectedly as a thief! Blessed are all who are watching for me, who keep their robes ready so they will not need to walk naked and ashamed."*
>
> *And they gathered all the rulers and their armies to a place called* Armageddon *in Hebrew.* (Revelation 16:12–16)

9. Why does the sixth angel pour out his bowl (verse 12)?

_____

_____

_____

_____

_____

10. For what reason are the rulers of the world gathering (verse 14)?

_____

_____

_____

_____

_____

About this supernatural event Tim LaHaye and Thomas Ice say, "God is clearly baiting the Antichrist and drawing him into His trap, which is set for further and final judgment at the second coming." [1]

Another big event signaling Armageddon (some think occurring at the time of Armageddon) is the destruction of New Babylon. Remember, the ancient city of Babylon *is* being rebuilt in Iraq. Revelation 17 and 18 describe the dramatic rise and fall of this city, which the Antichrist will use as his center of economic, political, and religious power (see also Isaiah 13–14; Jeremiah 50–51; and Zechariah 5:5–11).

11. Read Revelation 18 in your Bible. How does John describe Babylon's demise?

_____

_____

_____

_____

_____

> "Scriptures are not clear whether this destruction of Babylon is immediately before the Second Coming or immediately afterward. According to [Revelation] 16:19, however, the great earthquake that precedes the Second Coming will destroy the cities of the Gentiles, and it could be that Babylon [will be] destroyed at the same time." [2]
>
> John Walvoord

A third indicator of Armageddon's arrival is the national regeneration of Israel. Long predicted by the Hebrew prophets, the Jewish people as a whole will finally experience a spiritual awakening. They will embrace Christ as Messiah and enjoy the favor and protection of God. Zechariah recorded these events:

[Says the Lord]: "For my plan is to destroy all the nations that come against Jerusalem. Then I will pour out a spirit of grace and prayer on the family of David and on all the people of Jerusalem. They will look on me whom they have pierced and mourn for him as for an only son. They will grieve bitterly for him as for a firstborn son who has died."
(Zechariah 12:9–10)

12. What will happen when the Jews see the wrath of God on their enemies and experience God's gracious and merciful deliverance? Why is this significant?

_____

_____

_____

_____

_____

_____

Finding the Connection

(Armageddon, pp. 137–38)

The ways of God are mysterious. Who can truly fathom his love or completely understand his purposes or plans? Why does God do *what* he does, *how* he does, and *when* he does? Perhaps you've heard someone say, "I don't see why God just doesn't _____" or "Why does God allow _____?" Maybe you've made such comments yourself.

One scene in *Armageddon* touches on this difficulty of trusting in God's wisdom and power (especially when we don't see behind life's events to the eternal "why" or "how"). It features one of the main characters, Chang Wong, a young man who had been forced against his will to take the mark of the beast on his forehead. Chang hates this mark because it makes him—an ardent follower of Jesus—appear to be a worshiper of the Antichrist.

TSION TOOK CHANG BEHIND an outcropping of rock. "What can I do for you?"

Chang took off his cap, exposing the 30 emblazoned on his forehead and the thin, pink line where the Global Community biochip had been inserted. He caught the pity in the older man's eyes.

"I confess it is strange, Mr. Wong, to see that, when I also see the mark of the believer on you."

"I can't stand to look in the mirror," Chang said. "I don't dare take off my hat here. Yes, it may have kept me alive and yes, I had access where no believer would have dreamed. But it mocks me, curses me. I hate it."

"It was forced on you, son. It was not your choice or your fau—"

"I know all that, sir, but I want it gone. Is that possible?"

"I do not know."

"Sir, I study your teachings every day. You say that with God all things are possible. Why would he not remove this now?"

"I do not know, Chang. I just do not want to promise that he will."

"But what if I believe he will? And if you believe?"

"We can agree in faith on this, Chang, but as much as we believe and trust and study, no one can claim to know the mind of God. If you want me to pray that God will remove it, I will. And I believe he can and will do what he chooses. But I want you to pledge that you will accept his decision either way."

"Of course."

"Do not say that glibly. I can see how much you want this, and if God does not grant it, I do not want to see your faith threatened."

"I will be disappointed and I will wonder why, but I will accept it. Will you pray for me?"

Dr. Ben-Judah seemed to study Chang's face. He pressed his lips together, then looked away. Finally, he said, "I will. Come, sit over here and wait."

13. What was Chang's unique struggle as he lived during the Tribulation?

_____

_____

_____

_____

_____

_____

14. What situation or looming event have *you* had a hard time reconciling with the goodness and wisdom of God?

_____

_____

_____

15. How should Christians interpret "unanswered" prayers?

_____

As you will note in the highlighted box text, the problem of deception faced by Chang represents a specific example of a struggle against satanic deception that we all face. Whether our problems arise from disappointments over events we can't control or our inability to see or accept God's answers to our prayers, there are certainly spiritual principles that can help us remain faithful in the midst of deceiving circumstances.

"Deception will continue to increase as the end times approach. Consequently, it is imperative that God's people be well informed about what the future holds so they can avoid being deceived. We suggest the following six steps:

"A. *Know your Bible!* Jesus said that 'the truth shall make you free.' The Bible is the truth of God, so the better you know the Scriptures, the better prepared you will be to withstand Satan's deceptive ways. The daily reading of the Scriptures, particularly the New Testament, is a must for every Christian who would know truth. Study biblical prophecy, both from the Scriptures and from those prophecy scholars you trust.

"B. *Test the spirits! (1 John 4:1)* Everything comes down to whether a teaching agrees with the Scripture. That is why you should study the Bible regularly, so that you can test any new teaching by the Scripture. . . . Always ask, Does the message or teaching glorify Jesus? (See John 16:13–14). . . .

"C. *Seek God's guidance in life and teaching! (Proverbs 3:6)* The Lord wants to guide and direct His children. If you are willing to be led by God, He will guide you to truth.

"D. *Avoid immorality!* Nothing clouds the mind like lust and sin. They impair the reasoning of the mind on matters eternal.

"E. *Share your faith aggressively with others!* This world has never been more religiously confused. As you witness to others about your faith, you strengthen your own convictions and help many of those to whom you reach out.

"F. *Walk in the Spirit! (Ephesians 5:17–21)* All Christians in every age should walk in the Spirit, for Paul says that is 'the will of the Lord' (verse 17). As the Spirit fills and uses your life, He will make you sensitive to both truth and error." [3]

Tim LaHaye and Jerry Jenkins

Making the Change

One of the most intriguing and most discussed prophetic passages in the Old Testament is Ezekiel's vision of the valley of dry bones.

The LORD took hold of me, and I was carried away by the Spirit of the LORD to a valley filled with bones. He led me around among the old, dry bones that covered the valley floor. They were scattered everywhere across the ground. Then he asked me, "Son of man, can these bones become living people again?"

"O Sovereign LORD," I replied, "you alone know the answer to that."

Then he said to me, "Speak to these bones and say, 'Dry bones, listen to the word of the LORD! This is what the Sovereign LORD says: Look! I am going to breathe into you and make you live again! I will put flesh and muscles on you and cover you with skin. I will put breath into you, and you will come to life. Then you will know that I am the LORD.'"

So I spoke these words, just as he told me. Suddenly as I spoke, there was a rattling noise all across the valley. The bones of each body came together and attached themselves as they had been before. Then as I watched, muscles and flesh formed over the bones. Then skin formed to cover their bodies, but they still had no breath in them.

Then he said to me, "Speak to the winds and say: 'This is what the Sovereign LORD says: Come, O breath, from the four winds! Breathe into these dead bodies so that they may live again.'"

So I spoke as he commanded me, and the wind entered the bodies, and they began to breathe. They all came to life and stood up on their feet—a great army of them.

Then he said to me, "Son of man, these bones represent the people of Israel. They are say-ing, 'We have become old, dry bones—all hope is gone.' Now give them this message from the Sovereign LORD: O my people, I will open your graves of exile and cause you to rise again. Then I will bring you back to the land of Israel. When this happens, O my people, you will know that I am the LORD. I will put my Spirit in you, and you will live and return home to your own land. Then you will know that I am the LORD. You will see that I have done everything just as I promised. I, the LORD, have spoken!" (Ezekiel 37:1–14)

16. What details does this passage reveal about Israel's future spiritual regeneration?

_____

_____

_____

_____

_____

_____

_____

_____

"The *bones* represent hopeless and helpless Israel. The *graves* speak of her political demise. The *Spirit* is the Holy Spirit, who will effect the regeneration of the people. The vision does not depict the physical resurrection of individu-als, but the political (prior to the second coming of Christ) and spiritual (at the second coming of Christ) revivals of Israel." [4]

Charles Ryrie

---

17. If God can resurrect and restore a whole nation of stubborn people, what does that tell you about the divine possibilities in your life?

_____

_____

_____

_____

_____

_____

18. What "impossible situation" do you need to trust God with today?

_____

_____

_____

_____

_____

_____

Pursuing the Truth

In certain big ways, the future is set in stone. We know how the world will end. But in many smaller ways there is much uncertainty. *What about this friend or that relative?* we wonder. *Will he or she be ready to meet the Lord?*

19. How are you motivated to live today in light of these lessons? What actions can you change in order to live out this truth?

_____

_____

_____

_____

_____

_____

_____

20. Think of at least one memorable illustration of the following spiritual/theological concepts that you remember from what we've studied thus far or from the Left Behind stories.
the utter sinfulness of humanity _____

_____

_____

the faithfulness of God_____

_____

_____

the power and holiness of God _____

_____

_____

the need for faith _____

_____

_____

the importance of personal witness_____

_____

_____

Before tackling the question below, read Philippians 1:9–11:

I pray that your love for each other will overflow more and more, and that you will keep on growing in your knowledge and understanding. For I want you to understand what really matters, so that you may live pure and blameless lives until Christ returns. May you always be filled with the fruit of your salvation—those good things that are produced in your life by Jesus Christ—for this will bring much glory and praise to God.

21. How is Paul's almost two thousnd-year-old prayer for the Philippians an appropriate prayer for modern day believers?

_____

_____

_____

_____

_____

_____

22. Compose your own prayer that summarizes what you feel after this study.

_____

_____

_____

_____

_____

_____

Lesson in Review . . .

- As the great and terrible Battle of Armageddon draws near (heralding the second coming of Christ), several events will occur.
- The sixth Bowl Judgment will dry up the Euphrates River, allowing the vast armies of the east to march on Israel.
- The seventh Bowl Judgment—a cosmic earthquake—will shake the world.
- New Babylon, the headquarters of Antichrist, will be destroyed.
- Israel will *finally* embrace Christ as her Messiah and will experience salvation on a national level.

LEFT

BEHIND

Armageddon

Lesson 3
"In This Corner . . ."

1. How do you respond to the possibility that certain world leaders (and thus, the countries they rule) are controlled—or at least blinded and influenced—by Satan?

_____

_____

_____

_____

_____

2. Have you ever been in an armed conflict? What was that like?

_____

_____

_____

_____

_____

3. What is the most stunning battle scene you've seen on TV or in a movie? How does this compare to the biblical descriptions of Armageddon?

_____

_____

_____

_____

_____

Unfolding the Story

(*Armageddon,* pp. 297–300)

In the novel *Armageddon,* authors Tim LaHaye and Jerry Jenkins include an intriguing scene in which the Antichrist shares his dreams and goals. To the world he is a charismatic, sometimes ruthless man known as Global Community Potentate Nicolae Carpathia. In this passage, we see him for what he truly is, the God-hating incarnation of Satan, planning to lay waste to the nations of the world:

"YES, I WILL ADMIT IT. The father and the son have been my formidable foes over the generations. They have their favorites—the Jews, of all people. The Jews are the apples of the elder's eye, but therein lies his weakness. He has such a soft spot for them that they will be his undoing.

"My forces and I almost had them eradicated not so many generations ago, but father and son intervened, gave them back their own land, and foiled us again. Fate has toyed with us many times, my friends, but in the end we shall prevail.

"Father and son thought they were doing the world a favor by putting their intentions in writing. The whole plan is there, from sending the son to die and resurrect—which I proved I could do as well—to foretelling this entire period. Yes, many millions bought into this great lie. Up to now I would have to acknowledge that the other side has had the advantage.

"But two great truths will be their undoing. First, I know the truth. They are not greater or better than I or anyone else. They came from the same place we all did. And second, they must not have realized that I can read. I read their book! I know what they are up to! I know what happens next, and I even know where!

"Let them turn the lights off in the great city that I loved so much! Ah, how beautiful it was when it was the center for commerce and government, and the great ships and planes brought in goods from all over the globe. So it is dark now. And so what if it is eventually destroyed? I will build it back up, because I am more powerful than father and son combined.

"Let them shake the earth until it is level and drop hundred-pound chunks of ice from the skies. I will win in the end because I have read their battle plan. The old man plans to send the son to set up the kingdom he predicted more than three hundred times in his book, and he even tells where the son will land! Ladies and gentlemen, we will have a surprise waiting for him.

"The son and I have been battling for the souls of men and women from the beginning. If you rulers and I join forces from all over the world and act in unison from a single staging area, we can once and for all rid ourselves of those forces that have hindered our total victory up to now.

"The so-called Messiah loves the city of Jerusalem above all cities in the world. He even calls it the Eternal City. Well, we shall see about that. That is where he supposedly died and came back to life.

"This strange affection for the Jews resulted in what he tells them is an eternal covenant of blessing. If we, the rulers of the earth, combine all our resources and attack the Jews, the son has to come to their defense. That is when we turn our sights on him and eliminate him. That will give us total control of the earth, and we will be ready to take on the father for mastery of the universe."

Nicolae had made two rounds of the table and returned to his chair, looking spent. "It is in their Bible," he said. "And they claim never to lie. We know right where he will be. Are you with me?"

"We are with you, Excellency," the South American said, "but where will that be?"

"We rally everyone—all of our tanks and planes and weapons and armies—in the Plain of Megiddo. This area in northern Israel, also known as the Plain of Esdraelon or the Plain of Jezreel, is about thirty kilometers southeast of Haifa and one hundred kilometers north of Jerusalem. At the appointed time we will dispatch one-third of our forces to overrun the stronghold at Petra, and I shall do it this time without so much as one nuclear device. We shall overcome them with sheer numbers, perhaps even on horseback.

"The rest of our forces will march on the so-called Eternal City and blast through those infernal walls, destroying all the Jews. And that is where we shall be, joined by our victorious forces from Petra, in full force to surprise the son when he arrives. . . .

"Needless to say, we do not want or need to destroy the planet. We simply want your soldiers to have more than they need to wipe out the Jews and destroy the son I have so long opposed."

4. What are Nicolae's true intentions and ambitions?

_____

_____

_____

5. How well does he know the details of biblical prophecy?

_____

_____

_____

_____

_____

6. Why isn't Nicolae affected by the truth of God's superior wisdom and power—and the certainty of Christ's ultimate victory?

_____

_____

_____

_____

_____

Back to Reality

There has always been great speculation about which modern day nations will be "players" in the end-times drama foretold by the Bible. In the prelude to the big fight, imagine a global announcer coming on the loudspeaker with the traditional opening, "In this corner is . . ." followed by, "And in this corner we have . . ." Whom would he identify as the combatants siding with the Antichrist and who would be siding with God? The Bible contains some names with which we're familiar—Egypt, Ethiopia, Israel. But it also contains the cryptic names of mysterious nations—Cush, Gomer, Gog, and Magog. And some nations, like the United States, are not mentioned at all.

7. What nation or nations concern you the most—as far as their ambitions, intentions, etc.?

_____

_____

_____

_____

_____

8. Why do you think America seems to be "invisible" in all these prophetic, end-times passages?

_____

_____

_____

_____

_____

_____

9. Some Christians are critical of any concerted efforts to try to understand the biblical details regarding the end times. They argue that we should just trust God and keep serving him and stop obsessing over trying to figure out complicated and obscure prophetic passages. How do you respond to this argument, particularly in the light that America fits neatly in either corner of the prophetic final fight?

_____

_____

_____

_____

_____

_____

Understanding the Word

Will the Battle of Armageddon be a small affair, involving a handful of countries? Will it be a limited conflict? Consider the words of the prophet Joel:

> Say to the nations far and wide: "Get ready for war! Call out your best warriors! Let all your fighting men advance for the attack! Beat your plowshares into swords and your pruning hooks into spears. Train even your weaklings to be warriors. Come quickly, all you nations everywhere! Gather together in the valley."
> And now, O LORD, call out your warriors!
> "Let the nations be called to arms. Let them march to the valley of Jehoshaphat. There I, the LORD, will sit to pronounce judgment on them all. (Joel 3:9–12)

10. What does this passage say about the numbers involved? About the size of each nation's fighting force?

_____

_____

_____

_____

_____

Read through Psalm 2:

Why do the nations rage? Why do the people waste their time with futile plans? The kings of the earth prepare for battle; the rulers plot together against the LORD and against his anointed one. "Let us break their chains," they cry, "and free ourselves from this slavery."

But the one who rules in heaven laughs. The Lord scoffs at them. Then in anger he rebukes them, terrifying them with his fierce fury. For the LORD declares, "I have placed my chosen king on the throne in Jerusalem, my holy city."

The king proclaims the LORD's decree: "The LORD said to me, 'You are my son. Today I have become your Father. Only ask, and I will give you the nations as your inheritance, the ends of the earth as your possession. You will break them with an iron rod and smash them like clay pots.'"

Now then, you kings, act wisely! Be warned, you rulers of the earth! Serve the LORD with reverent fear, and rejoice with trembling. Submit to God's royal son, or he will become angry, and you will be destroyed in the midst of your pursuits—for his anger can flare up in an instant.

But what joy for all who find protection in him!

11. From these passages in Joel and Psalms, is the outcome of the battle in doubt? What biblical statements here support your answer?

_____

_____

_____

_____

_____

_____

12. What fate awaits those who foolishly cast their lot with Satan against God and his chosen people?

_____

_____

_____

_____

_____

13. What is the promise to those on God's side?

_____

_____

_____

_____

_____

"Although from their point of view they are gathered to fight it out for world power, the armies of the world will actually be assembled by Satan in anticipation of the second coming of Christ. The entire armed might of the world will be assembled in the Middle East, ready to contend with the power of Christ as he returns from heaven. As subsequent events make clear, the movement will be completely futile and hopeless. The armies of the world are by no means equipped to fight the armies of heaven. Still, Satan will assemble the nations for this final hour, and, in fact, the nations will choose to side with Satan and oppose the second coming of Christ. It will be the best that Satan can do."[1]

John F. Walvoord

Finding the Connection

(*Armageddon*, pp. 206–8)

Many Christians watch the nightly news and are overcome with a sense of doom and gloom. It certainly does seem as though the world "is going to hell in a handbasket." The world and its troubles aside, what about when our own personal lives are unraveling and the ground beneath our souls seems shaky? Sometimes we are tempted to wonder, *Where is God? Why doesn't he act? Jesus promised to be with me but I can't sense his presence. Will I make it?*

Authors LaHaye and Jenkins include a scene in *Armageddon* that addresses all these concerns and questions. Chloe, one of the main characters in the Left Behind series, has been captured and jailed by the forces of Carpathia. She seems destined for execution, and her soul is troubled. Watch what happens next!

IT WAS THE MIDDLE OF THE EVENING in Illinois, and Chloe was surprised to have been left alone for hours. She had been right about solitary. The stairs led below ground, and she had been ushered into a small cell with no cot, no sink, no toilet, no chair, no bench, no nothing. Including no light or window. The duct tape had been removed from her mouth, and when the solid metal door was shut, she was in pitch darkness.

A small square hole in the door opened and was filled with Jock's face. "I'm going to let you get some rest," he said, "and I'm going to get some, too. Think about anything you can tell me that will benefit you, because when I come back, we're going to see if we need to give you an injection to help you open up. Your little shenanigans today bought you this. You're not going to like it in there if you're claustrophobic or afraid of the dark."

Chloe was both, but she was not about to admit it. She feared she would panic or go mad, but as she heard Jock's footsteps retreat, she was overcome with a sense of peace. "Thank you, Lord," she said. "I need you. I'm willing to die, but I don't want to shame you. I need you to override the truth serum. Don't let me give away anything or anybody, and keep me strong so I won't worry so much about myself. Help me keep my mind, my focus, and my priorities. And be with Kenny and Buck and Dad."

Just thinking about them brought a sob to her throat. Chloe pressed her back against the wall and lowered herself to the cold floor. "God, please, bring to mind Scriptures you want me to hear right now. Don't let hunger or fatigue or fear keep me from remembering. You know who I am and who I'm not. I just want to be what you want me to be. You know better than I that you're working with imperfection here."

She lay on her side with no heart palpitations from the closed-in space or the darkness. That alone was evidence that God was hearing her. She began rehearsing in her mind her memory verses, starting as far back in the Bible as she could remember. But when she stalled, she panicked. "Lord, keep my mind fresh. Don't let me forget. I want to be quoting you when I see you."

Her mind became a jumble. *How will I remember? What if my mind goes blank?* "Lord, please."

And suddenly, light. Was she dreaming? She blinked. The rusted, filthy chamber was bright enough to make her shield her eyes. A vision? A dream? A hallucination?

Then a voice. Quoting her favorite verses. She repeated them, word for word. "Is this your answer, God? You'll speak them and I'll repeat them? Thank you! Thank you!"

Loud banging on the door. "Keep it down in there!"

"Yes, peace, be still." That voice came from the corner!

Chloe pulled her hands from her eyes and jumped at a figure, sitting, a finger to his lips.

"Is it you, Lord?" she said, breathless.

"No one can see God and live," he whispered.

"Then who are you?"

"He sent me."

"Praise God."

"Yes, please."

"Can anyone else see you?"

"Tomorrow. Not until then."

"You'll remind me of what God has promised?"

"I will."

"You make me want to sing.". . . Chloe began singing. "When we walk with the Lord in the light of his word, what a glory he sheds on our way! While we do his good will, he abides with us still, and with all who will trust and obey."

"Shut up in there!"

Chloe sang louder: "Trust and obey, for there's no other way to be happy in Jesus, but to trust and obey. . . . Then in fellowship sweet we shall sit at his feet. . . ."

That brought knocking—it sounded like with a stick—and Chloe laughed aloud. "They don't like my voice," she told her new friend.

"Or the words," he said, and she laughed all the more.

14. How did God comfort Chloe in her moment of trial?

_____

_____

_____

_____

_____

15. How do each of the following actions help *you* in troubling, uncertain times?

praying _____

_____

quoting memorized Scripture _____

_____

singing worship songs _____

_____

16. Have you ever had an experience similar to Chloe's? What were your circumstances? What finally happened?

_____

_____

_____

_____

Making the Change

Psalm 31 is David's prayer for help in a time of desperate trouble. The exact situation is unknown, only that David was surrounded by enemies, much as Israel will one day be. Read the psalm and let God speak words of assurance to you:

> *O LORD, I have come to you for protection; don't let me be put to shame. Rescue me, for you always do what is right. Bend down and listen to me; rescue me quickly. Be for me a great rock of safety, a fortress where my enemies cannot reach me.*
>
> *You are my rock and my fortress. For the honor of your name, lead me out of this peril. Pull me from the trap my enemies set for me, for I find protection in you alone. I entrust my spirit into your hand. Rescue me, LORD, for you are a faithful God.*
>
> *I hate those who worship worthless idols. I trust in the LORD. I am overcome with joy because of your unfailing love, for you have seen my troubles, and you care about the anguish of my soul. You have not handed me over to my enemy but have set me in a safe place.*
>
> *Have mercy on me, LORD, for I am in distress. My sight is blurred because of my tears. My body and soul are withering away. I am dying from grief; my years are shortened by*

sadness. Misery has drained my strength; I am wasting away from within. I am scorned by all my enemies and despised by my neighbors—even my friends are afraid to come near me. When they see me on the street, they turn the other way. I have been ignored as if I were dead, as if I were a broken pot. I have heard the many rumors about me, and I am surrounded by terror. My enemies conspire against me, plotting to take my life.

*But I am trusting you, O L*ORD*, saying, "You are my God!" My future is in your hands. Rescue me from those who hunt me down relentlessly. Let your favor shine on your servant. In your unfailing love, save me. Don't let me be disgraced, O L*ORD*, for I call out to you for help. Let the wicked be disgraced; let them lie silent in the grave. May their lying lips be silenced—those proud and arrogant lips that accuse the godly.*

Your goodness is so great! You have stored up great blessings for those who honor you. You have done so much for those who come to you for protection, blessing them before the watching world. You hide them in the shelter of your presence, safe from those who conspire against them. You shelter them in your presence, far from accusing tongues.

*Praise the L*ORD*, for he has shown me his unfailing love. He kept me safe when my city was under attack. In sudden fear I had cried out, "I have been cut off from the L*ORD*!" But you heard my cry for mercy and answered my call for help.*

*Love the L*ORD*, all you faithful ones! For the L*ORD* protects those who are loyal to him, but he harshly punishes all who are arrogant. So be strong and take courage, all you who put your hope in the L*ORD*!*

17. What insights does this psalm give you into the character of God?

_____

_____

_____

_____

_____

18. In what new ways does David's example encourage and challenge you to respond when troubles converge on your life?

_____

_____

_____

_____

Pursuing the Truth

Given the recent experiences with terrorism that America has experienced, followed by the war in Afghanistan and then the war in Iraq, the attention of the world seems riveted on the Middle East. We may not be able to identify all the participants in the climactic events of history, but we can't keep our eyes off the lands that surround the tiny land of Israel. There seems little doubt that when the bell for the battle rings, one corner will definitely be occupied by the people God calls his own.

19. Review Revelation 16:12–14. Note the phrase "the kings of the east" marching across the dry Euphrates riverbed toward Armageddon. What nations might these be?

_____

_____

_____

_____

"These 'kings of the east' have befuddled Bible prophecy scholars for many years, for few scholars mentioned anything about them. That is, until the communist takeover of China after World War II. Since then it has become apparent that this largest of all countries (by population) has a prophetic role, however minor it may be, in end-time events. While China had been content to stay within its vast borders for thousands of years and keep largely to itself, its communist dictators have changed all that. They seem to have the same obsession that characterized Communists before them—world conquest. . . .

"No longer is China the paper tiger she was for almost five thousand years. In our lifetime she has startled the world and frightened many in the military complex with her enormous economic and military potential. Many observers recognize that within ten or, at most, twenty years, China could very well threaten the entire world, even more than the Soviet Union did just a decade ago."[2]

Tim LaHaye and Jerry Jenkins

---

20. How have vivid scenes from the war in Iraq helped you visualize the details of this march against Israel?

_____

_____

_____

_____

21. Consider carefully the following chart and comments. How do you respond to the possibility of a major conflict involving Israel that is not, in fact, Armageddon yet?

_____

_____

_____

_____

Though many Bible students see the battle/invasion described in Ezekiel 38–39 as the final Battle of Armageddon, there are good reasons to see them as separate conflicts. Consider the differences:

Gog & Magog (Ezekiel 38–39)	Armageddon (Revelation 19:11–21)
Israel has some allies	The whole world opposes Israel
Israel living securely	Israel on the run and in hiding
Invasion from the north	Invasion from every direction
Goal is to plunder and take spoil (38:6)	Goal is the destruction of the Jews
Enemies destroyed by a series of catastrophes	Enemies destroyed by the second coming of Christ!
Ends on the mountains of Israel	Ends on the plains of Meggido

Ponder the following statements designed to help you see the differences between the two conflicts of Gog and Magog and Armageddon.

"We believe that the participants of the battle of Gog and Magog can be identified by tracing the migration of those ancient peoples to their modern-day descendants. Ezekiel says this battle will occur 'in the latter years' (38:8) and 'in the last days' (38:16). The invasion involves a coalition headed by 'Gog of the land of Magog, the prince of Rosh, Meshech and Tubal' (38:2). Magog has been identified as ancient terminology for the area including modern-day Russia, Ukraine, and Kazakhstan. Ezekiel further identifies Magog as coming from 'the remote parts of the north' (38:6).

"Gog will lead the invasion of Israel, and Ezekiel 38:5–6 adds that other nations will join with Gog—Persia (Iran), Ethiopia or Cush (Sudan), Put (Libya), and Gomer and Beth-togarmah (Turkey). Sheba and Dedan in Ezekiel 38:13 refer to Saudi Arabia. All the allies of Magog are reasonably well identified and they are all presently Muslim.

Interestingly, such an alignment of nations is already configured on the world scene today, so such an invasion does not seem like a far-fetched possibility." [3]

Tim LaHaye & Thomas Ice

"God will permit the nations named in Ezekiel 38 to unite together to accomplish their evil purpose. It is very possible that these nations will attack under the banner of Islam. But God also promised that he will destroy those nations just when victory seems to be within their grasp. His purpose for doing this is to reveal to the world that the God of the Bible, not the god of Islam, is the one true God. . . .

"So what should be our response to Muslims today? Should we view them as enemies? Should we respond to the events of September 11 by lashing back in anger at those who share the religion of the terrorists? No! For to do so is to deny the love and power of God. . . . I have not come across any passage of Scripture that says the Great Commission excludes Muslims. They need Jesus Christ. The end times will come according to God's own schedule. The battle described in Ezekiel 38–39 will take place. And it is very possible that the nations involved will be united because of their common belief in Islamic fundamentalism. In the meantime, we have a mission to accomplish. That mission is to preach Jesus Christ, God's Son, crucified, raised from the dead, victorious, and coming again. Salvation is found only in his name." [4]

Samuel Naaman

22. What particular truths have you gleaned from this study? How do you expect to apply them in your life this week?

_____

_____

_____

_____

_____

Lesson in Review . . .

- In accordance with God's sovereign plan for the ages, Antichrist will successfully rally all the nations of the world to attack Israel at the end of the Tribulation.
- This final Battle of Armageddon is not to be confused with an earlier, unsuccessful attack on Israel, occurring after the Rapture and described in Ezekiel 38–39.

LEFT

BEHIND

Armageddon

Lesson 4
Surrounded!

1. Describe a time in your life when you felt really helpless and hopeless. What happened?

_____

_____

_____

_____

_____

_____

2. Technology has made events such as the 2003 war in Iraq a "real-time" experience for people all over the world. How did you respond to the fluctuating positive and negative news that came out of the coverage of that war?

_____

_____

_____

_____

✔ *Unfolding the Story*
(*Armageddon,* pp. 341–42)

Toward the end of the eleventh novel in the Left Behind series, readers are propelled at breakneck speed toward the great and terrible Battle of Armageddon. God's people are holed up at Petra, and the nation of Israel faces overwhelming, seemingly impossible odds:

THE SHEER NUMBER OF TROOPS swelled well beyond the Valley of Megiddo and spilled north and south and east and west, past Jerusalem and down toward Edom. Some estimates included an almost unimaginable mounted army alone of more than two hundred thousand. Aerial views shot by GCNN aircraft could show only a million or so troops at a time, but dozens and dozens of separate such pictures were broadcast.

Chang sensed panic on the part of the people at Petra. Those who saw the news could not imagine standing against such an overwhelming force. Those who didn't see the news heard it from others, and the word swept the camp. Many ran to the high places and could make out the clouds of dust and the dark masses of humanity, beasts, and weaponry slowly making their way across the desert.

Chaim took the occasion to call the people together, just before the evening manna was expected. "My dear people, brothers and sisters in Messiah. Be of good cheer. Fear not. I am hearing wonderful reports out of Jerusalem, where our brother Tsion preaches the gospel of Jesus Christ with great boldness and, I am happy to report, great results as well.

"I only ten minutes ago talked with a very exhausted and still very busy Cameron Williams. He tells me thousands are repenting of their sins and turning to Christ, acknowledging Jesus of Nazareth as Messiah. Praise the Lord God Almighty, maker of heaven and earth!"

The people seemed encouraged and cheered and wept and raised their hands.

"We are not ignorant," Chaim continued, "of what is to come. New Babylon has fallen, utterly destroyed in one hour, fulfilling the prophecies. That leaves only two events on the prophetic calendar, my friends. The first is?"

And the people shouted, "The seventh Bowl Judgment!"

"And the second, oh, praise God!"

"The Glorious Appearing!"

Chaim concluded, "We serve the great God of Abraham, Isaac, and Jacob, the deliverer of Shadrach, Meshach, and Abednego. We lived through the fires of the Antichrist, and we have been delivered from the snare of the fowler. Do not be afraid. Stand still, and see the salvation of the Lord, which he will accomplish for you. For the enemy whom you see today, you shall soon see no more forever. The Lord will fight for you, and you shall hold your peace."

3. Who or what is the "enemy" Chaim refers to? What effect does this enemy's approach have on the believers in the novel?

_____

_____

_____

_____

_____

_____

4. When this event takes place, what two significant "dates" are left on God's prophetic calendar?

_____

_____

_____

_____

_____

5. What Old Testament stories does Chaim cite to encourage the people?

_____

_____

_____

_____

_____

"Can you imagine all the manpower, all the strategies, all the work that will go into the Antichrist's efforts to bring all the great armies of the world to Armageddon? And behind the scenes, it's actually God who will orchestrate every detail of the event. Proverbs 21:1 tells us, 'The king's heart is like channels of water in the hands of the Lord; He turns it wherever He wishes.' Though at first it may not seem like it, God will be in full control of all that happens. And in the end, he will turn the battle of Armageddon to his advantage for a clear and dramatic victory over all the forces of Antichrist." [1]

Tim LaHaye and Thomas Ice

Back to Reality

There is never a time when the Middle East is *not* a powder keg, fluctuating between simmering and exploding. The situation in and around Israel is always volatile, and just about any event could trigger something huge. Global alliances and rifts make it possible to envision the destructive biblical scenario at some time in the future. It isn't difficult to imagine how the deep-seated hatred or the use of certain weapons in the Middle East could lead to hostilities that would involve the entire world.

6. What are some of the typical (nonbiblical) explanations or causes people give for the continual smoldering tensions in the Middle East?

_____

_____

_____

_____

_____

_____

_____

_____

"The word *Armageddon* refers to a place in northern Israel, which in English means the 'Mount of Megiddo.' It is pictured in prophecy as the marshaling point for a great army in the end time just before the second coming of Christ. This led many to believe that the Gulf War was the prelude to Armageddon.

"Most intelligent investigators soon realized this war was not precisely what the Bible predicted, because Armageddon will occur in Israel and the Gulf War concerned the nation of Kuwait. Nevertheless there was a worldwide sense of impending climax, which soon dissipated when the Gulf War was over.

"Yet events following the Gulf War have left the world in an uncertain situation, with Syria acquiring arms sufficient to destroy Israel completely. Iran and Iraq also have weapons of destruction. It would only take one attack to plunge the world into major chaos and a world conflict. Deterring all this is the fact that Israel itself is well armed with nuclear weapons and is able to reply in kind." [2]

John Walvoord

7. How much do you worry about world events? What specifically concerns you right now? How do you think you might feel if you were an Israeli citizen today? a Palestinian? a Muslim from one of the other neighboring countries?

_____

_____

_____

_____

_____

8. If you had an opportunity now to visit the Holy Land, would you? Why or why not? If so, what would you most like to see?

_____

_____

_____

_____

_____

Understanding the Word

God's Word is the ultimate rock of safety. It is our anchor in the storm. In the pages of Scripture we find both assurance and reassurance. We are repeatedly reminded of God's absolute power. We see his perfect faithfulness to his people over and over again. To paraphrase the words of the old spiritual, God may make his children wait, but he will *never* be too late.

Psalm 2:4 reminds us that when the enemies of God (and God's people) plot and scheme, God just laughs. Why? Because human ploys are futile in the face of God's limitless power. Other passages remind us of God's omnipotence:

- "Is anything too hard for the LORD?" (Genesis 18:14)
- "O Sovereign LORD! You have made the heavens and earth by your great power. Nothing is too hard for you!" (Jeremiah 32:17)
- "I am the LORD, the God of all the peoples of the world. Is anything too hard for me?" (Jeremiah 32:27)

9. How do passages like these encourage you and strengthen your faith? How can you apply them to daily living?

_____

_____

_____

_____

_____

10. Consider God's past protection of and care for Israel—the miraculous Exodus from Egyptian bondage under Moses, the return from Babylonian captivity, the Old Testament story of Esther, the preservation of the nation through other modern genocidal efforts (Hitler's Holocaust). What does this say to you about God? About his commitment to his people?

_____

_____

_____

_____

_____

"Though many teachers of prophecy make dire predictions about the destruction of the world, the fact is that Bible prophecy does not say the world will be completely destroyed by nuclear weapons. The destruction described in the book of Revelation is largely supernatural, through earthquakes, disruption of the heavens, famine, pestilence, and so forth. Apparently God will control the evil in the world sufficiently so that the world will not destroy itself before the appointed prophetic climax." [3]

John Walvoord

In Luke 21, Jesus teaches his followers about Israel's future—both near and far. His words foreshadowed the imminent destruction of Jerusalem by the Romans (A.D. 70), as well as the future last-days invasion by Gentile armies:

And when you see Jerusalem surrounded by armies, then you will know that the time of its destruction has arrived. Then those in Judea must flee to the hills. Let those in Jerusalem escape, and those outside the city should not enter it for shelter. For those will be days of God's vengeance, and the prophetic words of the Scriptures will be fulfilled. How terrible it will be for pregnant women and for mothers nursing their babies. For there will be great distress in the land and wrath upon this people. They will be brutally killed by the sword or sent away as captives to all the nations of the world. And Jerusalem will be conquered and trampled down by the Gentiles until the age of the Gentiles comes to an end.

And there will be strange events in the skies—signs in the sun, moon, and stars. And down here on earth the nations will be in turmoil, perplexed by the roaring seas and strange tides. The courage of many people will falter because of the fearful fate they see coming upon the earth, because the stability of the very heavens will be broken up. Then everyone will see the Son of Man arrive on the clouds with power and great glory. So when all these things begin to happen, stand straight and look up, for your salvation is near! (Luke 21:20–28)

11. How would you describe the tone of Jesus' words here? Hopeful? Somber? Triumphant? Other?

_____

_____

_____

12. What directions did he give the disciples about how believers were to respond to these events?

_____

_____

_____

Finding the Connection

Supernatural intervention is not just grist for a best-selling series of novels or a surprising event reserved for the end of the world. God has a long track record of coming to the aid of his people when they are in trouble. In the Old Testament we read the story of the children of Israel, poised on the edge of entering the Promised Land. Facing the daunting prospect of conquering its well-armed inhabitants, Moses said:

When you go out to fight your enemies and you face horses and chariots and an army greater than your own, do not be afraid. The LORD your God, who brought you safely out of Egypt, is with you! Before you go into battle, the priest will come forward to speak with the troops. He will say, "Listen to me, all you men of Israel! Do not be afraid as you go out to fight today! Do not lose heart or panic. For the LORD your God is going with you! He will fight for you against your enemies, and he will give you victory!" (Deuteronomy 20:1–5)

13. What is the main point repeated in Moses' speech to the Israelites? Why is an awareness of God's presence important to the people of God, at any time and in any place?

_____

_____

_____

_____

_____

_____

14. To what degree are you convinced that God is always with you?

_____

_____

_____

_____

_____

_____

15. How can we be assured of God's protection and presence when we can't *sense* his nearness? (See Psalm 139:1–12; Matthew 28:20; Hebrews 13:5.)

_____

_____

_____

_____

_____

_____

Making the Change

(*Armageddon*, p. 351)

Perhaps it is spiritual blindness. Certainly it is foolish pride. Whatever the case, the enemies of God relentlessly pursue God's people even though they cannot ultimately win. In this scene from *Armageddon*, authors LaHaye and Jenkins do a good job of portraying the astounding arrogance of Antichrist. His violent hatred will cloud his ability to remember God's promises to protect his people with the greatest power in the universe.

UNABLE TO SLEEP, Chang made his way to the tech center and his computer at about four in the morning. Idly checking the GCNN affiliate feed out of Haifa, he heard a report of troop deployments.

"Supreme Potentate Nicolae Carpathia has made no secret of his strategy," the reporter intoned. "In fact, it seems as if he would just as soon enemy targets know what's coming. I spoke with him late last night at his bunker, somewhere near the Sea of Galilee."

"You see," Carpathia said, "we have such an overwhelming advantage in manpower, firepower, and technology, it really makes little difference what we encounter. I have not hidden that we have two main objectives aiming toward the same goal. We want to lay siege to the city of Jerusalem, where the majority of the remaining Jews reside. And we want to eliminate Petra once and for all, where what they like to call 'the Remnant' remains in hiding like scared children.

"They know we are coming, and they will see us coming, and there is little they can do about it."

16. What's wrong with Carpathia's thinking? What facts does he fail to consider?

_____

_____

_____

_____

_____

The viewpoint taken in the Left Behind series and in these Bible study guides is that Christians will be raptured (i.e., taken up into heaven) *before* the events of the Tribulation. If that is true, then believers doing these Bible lessons will not even be on earth at the time of

Armageddon. (Unless you happen to stumble on a copy of this workbook after some of these events have occurred!) Even so, there are valuable principles for our lives today that we can glean from our study.

17. In this lesson we have been reminded of God's long and faithful history of coming to the aid of his people. He is a good God, a loving Father, and a strong Savior. He never forsakes his children. What does this truth mean to you in the context of the unique situations you are facing right now?

_____

_____

_____

_____

_____

_____

_____

18. In what ways are you tempted to doubt God's power or his desire to "show up" in your life and meet your needs?

_____

_____

_____

_____

_____

_____

_____

_____

"Prophecy enhances our understanding of the character of God and leads us to worship him. Over and over again in his letters, Paul became so overwhelmed with God's character that he couldn't help but worship when he considered God's powerful plan." [4]

Tony Evans

Pursuing the Truth

19. In 1 John 4:4, we find these words, "The Spirit who lives in you is greater than the spirit who lives in the world." How is this promise a comfort in tough, trying, or terrifying times?

_____

_____

_____

_____

_____

The Old Testament records an incident in which Moab and Ammon launched a surprise attack on King Jehoshaphat and the nation of Judah. Filled with fear, Jehoshaphat proclaimed a national fast, gathered all the people, and then prayed:

> *"O our God, won't you stop them? We are powerless against this mighty army that is about to attack us. We do not know what to do, but we are looking to you for help."* (2 Chronicles 20:12)

20. What qualities make this a "model prayer" for believers in uncertain or distressing situations?

_____

_____

_____

_____

_____

21. Isaiah 26:3–4 says, "You will keep in perfect peace all who trust in you, whose thoughts are fixed on you! Trust in the LORD always, for the LORD GOD is the eternal Rock." According to this passage, what is the secret to having inner peace?

_____

_____

_____

_____

22. What do you have in common with the future end-times people of God, who will find themselves surrounded at Armageddon by fierce enemies?

_____

_____

_____

_____

_____

23. What insight about God from this lesson is most encouraging to you today?

_____

_____

_____

_____

_____

"The God who is totally sovereign over the future is the same God who cares about you and knows your personal future. Is there anything in your future that you are worried about? Give your concerns to him in prayer . . . right now. Why hold your problems in your hands when you can place them in his hands?" [5]

Tim LaHaye and Thomas Ice

Lesson in Review. . .

- The massive, seemingly invincible forces of Antichrist will converge on Israel at Armageddon, determined to exterminate every living follower of God.
- Humanly speaking, the people of God will stand no chance of resisting this devastating attack.
- Believers serve an awesome God who is good, who is all-powerful, and who always keeps his promises.
- The One who is with and in believers is greater than anyone or anything else!

LEFT

BEHIND

Armageddon

Lesson 5
The Arrival of the King

1. A late-night television talk show once featured a recurring segment called "Brushes with Greatness." Selected audience members would stand and relate their funny and strange real-life encounters with the rich and famous. If you were asked, what celebrities or well-known individuals have you met or seen "up close and personal"? What made meeting them memorable?

_____

_____

_____

_____

_____

_____

2. Why do you think we are so fascinated by the famous and powerful people of our time?

_____

_____

_____

_____

_____

"Some news stories are so enormous that ordinary headlines and bold print just won't cut it. For outsized events and cataclysmic happenings, newspapers for decades have resorted to what came to be known as 'Second Coming type'— that is, a style and size of lettering that jumps off the page, grabs a reader by the throat, and demands, READ ME!

"Second Coming type has been used to announce such major events as the Allied victory over Hitler, the end of World War II, and even (in one of the biggest blunders in American journalism history) Thomas Dewey's 'defeat' of Harry S. Truman in the 1948 presidential election.

"But why give the name 'Second Coming type' to the fonts used for such tremendous events? Why not just call it Big News type or Major Event type or Can You Believe *This?* type?

"The reason, of course, is that there *is* no bigger event than the second coming of Christ, and even the most irreligious journalist at the most liberal newspaper in the most ungodly city in the world knows it. Ironically, when he comes, Second Coming type will sit unused on the presses. Why? Because there will be no time left to put out a flash street edition to announce his return!" [1]

Tim LaHaye and Jerry Jenkins

Unfolding the Story

(*Armageddon*, pp. 276–78)

The novel *Armageddon* takes us through the final part of the Great Tribulation, the terrible period when Antichrist wreaks havoc upon the earth. In the following scene, Tsion Ben-Judah, a great spokesman for the faith, reviews what has happened and previews what is about to happen:

"GOD HAS LAID ON MY HEART a message that I believe he would have me share with you," Tsion began. "I shall not whitewash or sugarcoat it, as we are at the most perilous time in the history of mankind. We are nearly into the last six months of life as we know it. The battle of the ages that has raged since the beginning of time is about to reach its climax.

"The evil ruler of this world, the Antichrist, is spewing his anger and vengeance primarily on God's chosen people. All over the world innocent men and women are being tortured, even as we speak. Their crime? They are Jewish. Some are believers in Jesus as Messiah, and many are not. Regardless, they refuse the mark of loyalty to Nicolae Carpathia, and he makes them pay every day.

"You have seen the footage, and you know the glee with which the Evil One watches his plan carried out.

"Many years ago I began proving the truth of God's Word by telling you in advance of the judgments and plagues to come, things clearly prophesied hundreds, yea thousands of years ago. We saw the fruition of the prophecy of a rider on a white horse, promising peace but bringing a sword. The red horse, World War III, followed that. That brought the black horse of famine, then the ashen horse of death. Next came the martyrdom of many saints before the Wrath of the Lamb earthquake.

"Those six judgments had been foretold in Scripture, and the seventh ushered in the next seven. Hail and fire rained on the earth. Then the burning mountain fell into the sea. Wormwood poisoned the waters, and then the sun, moon, and stars were dimmed by one-third. Demonic locusts attacked those who were not sealed by God, and then we were plagued by an army, two hundred million strong, of demonic horsemen who slew much of the population. The fourteenth judgment ushered in the last seven, five of which have already befallen us.

"Millions suffered from boils, and then the sea turned to blood, then the rivers. The sun scorched people to death and burned a third of the earth's greenery. The darkness that has fallen on New Babylon has been defended, rationalized, and explained away. But no one can account for the fact that it is so pervasive that it causes those caught in it to gnaw their tongues from the pain.

"Many have speculated how long this will last. I tell you nothing in Scripture indicates it will abate before the end. That is why the ruler of this world has moved out of his own kingdom. He may think the day will come when he and his people can move back in, but I proclaim he never will. Two more judgments await before the glorious appearing of our Lord and Savior, Jesus the Christ.

"Hear me! The Euphrates River will become as dry land! Scoff today but be amazed when it happens, and remember it was foretold. The last judgment will be an earthquake that levels the entire globe. This judgment will bring hail so huge it will kill millions.

"I am asked every day, how can people see all these things and still choose Antichrist over Christ? It is the puzzle of the ages. For many of you, it is already too late to change your mind. You may now see that you have chosen the wrong side in this war. But if you pledged your allegiance to the enemy of God by taking his mark of loyalty, it is too late for you.

"If you have not taken the mark yet, it may still be too late, because you waited so long. You pushed the patience of God past the breaking point.

"But there may be a chance for you. You will know only if you pray to receive Christ, tell God you recognize that you are a sinner and separated from him, and that you acknowledge that your only hope is in the blood of Christ, shed on the cross for you.

"Remember this: If you do not turn to Christ and are not saved from the coming judgment, this awful earth you endure right now is as good as your life will ever get. If you do turn to Christ and your heart has not already been hardened, this world is the worst you'll see for the rest of eternity.

"For those of you who are already my brothers and sisters in Christ around the world, I urge you to be faithful unto death, for Jesus himself said, 'Do not fear any of those things which you are about to suffer. Indeed, the devil is about to throw some of you into prison, that you may be tested. . . . Be faithful until death, and I will give you the crown of life.'

"What a promise! Christ himself will give you the crown of life. It shall be a thrill to see Jesus come yet again, but oh, what a privilege to die for his sake."

3. Which of the judgments described by Tsion sounds the worst to you, and why?

_____

_____

_____

_____

_____

_____

4. Tsion spoke of pushing "the patience of God past the breaking point" and it being "too late" for some. What did he mean by this?

_____

_____

_____

_____

_____

_____

5. How is it that some people can see obvious, inexplicable miracles and still resist and reject God?

_____

_____

_____

_____

_____

6. Tsion is an articulate spokesman for Christ—well able to explain God's words and works. How would you rate yourself when it comes to helping others understand spiritual truth?

_____

_____

_____

_____

_____

Back to Reality

It is difficult to describe life's ultimate realities, isn't it? How does one describe *love?* Or *faith?* How about *eternity?*

Reading Revelation, we are struck at times by John's obvious struggle to put into words the amazing end-times scenes to which he was given access. The authors of the Left Behind books do an admirable job of trying to imagine how all these events might actually unfold.

7. Who is your favorite Bible teacher or preacher? What qualities or abilities make that person your favorite?

_____

_____

_____

_____

_____

8. Do you have a favorite passage from the book *Armageddon*? If so, what is it, and why?

_____

_____

_____

_____

_____

_____

9. When was the last time you were absolutely gripped and riveted by a sermon or book—and compelled to make significant changes in your life? Explain.

_____

_____

_____

_____

_____

_____

"The second coming of Jesus Christ to earth will be no quiet manger scene. It will be the most dramatic and shattering event in the entire history of the universe. His coming in power and glory will seize the attention of the entire world." [2]

John F. Walvoord

Understanding the Word

Perhaps the single most famous passage about the return of Christ and the decisive battle of Armageddon is from Revelation 19. Here is what John saw:

Then I saw heaven opened, and a white horse was standing there. And the one sitting on the horse was named Faithful and True. For he judges fairly and then goes to war. His eyes were bright like flames of fire, and on his head were many crowns. A name was written on him, and only he knew what it meant. He was clothed with a robe dipped in blood, and his title was the Word of God. The armies of heaven, dressed in pure white linen, followed him on white horses. From his mouth came a sharp sword, and with it he struck down the nations. He ruled them with an iron rod, and he trod the winepress of the fierce wrath of almighty God. On his robe and thigh was written this title: King of kings and Lord of lords.

Then I saw an angel standing in the sun, shouting to the vultures flying high in the sky: "Come! Gather together for the great banquet God has prepared. Come and eat the flesh of kings, captains, and strong warriors; of horses and their riders; and of all humanity, both free and slave, small and great."

Then I saw the beast gathering the kings of the earth and their armies in order to fight against the one sitting on the horse and his army. And the beast was captured, and with him the false prophet who did mighty miracles on behalf of the beast—miracles that deceived all who had accepted the mark of the beast and who worshiped his statue. Both the beast and his false prophet were thrown alive into the lake of fire that burns with sulfur. Their entire army was killed by the sharp sword that came out of the mouth of the one riding the white horse. And all the vultures of the sky gorged themselves on the dead bodies. (Revelation 19:11–21)

10. Identify the names and titles ascribed to Christ in this passage. What is the significance of each?

_____

_____

_____

_____

_____

_____

11. What do you observe about the garments worn by Christ (verses 12–13)?

_____

_____

_____

"[Revelation 19:11–21] calls Jesus a righteous Judge, a righteous Warrior, and a righteous King. He is accompanied by the armies of heaven—but they are dressed as no other army in history. Usually soldiers are clothed in camouflage fatigues, but here they are all in white, symbolizing both their purity and Jesus' unconcern that their 'uniforms' would be soiled. There is no fear of this, for they will not lift a finger in the battle to come; Jesus will accomplish all by the power of his almighty word."[3]

Tim LaHaye and Jerry Jenkins

12. What weapons does Christ have, and how are they described?

13. What is the fate/destiny of those opposed to Christ?

"This is a terrifying picture of judgment, of God's wrath poured out on sinful man. The slaughter is beyond our comprehension, armies with hundreds of millions of troops wiped out in a single blast from the mouth of Jesus Christ." [4]

Tony Evans

Finding the Connection

(*Armageddon,* pp. 264–65)

Near the end of *Armageddon* (we hope that we are not spoiling the surprise of any Left Behind readers!), some departed Christians are being eulogized by friends and loved ones. Their memorial service serves as a challenge to us:

"[B]OTH ALBIE AND CHLOE were people of the Word. Oh, how they loved God's love letter to them and to us! Albie would be the first to tell you he was not a scholar, hardly a reader. He was a man of street smarts, knowledgeable in the ways of the world, quick and shrewd and sharp. But whenever the occasion arose when he could sit under the teaching of the Bible, he took notes, he asked questions, he drank it in. The Word of God was worked out in his life. It changed him. It helped mold him into the man he was the day he died.

"And Chloe, our dear sister and one of the original members of the tiny Tribulation Force that has grown so large today. Who could know her and not love her spirit, her mind, her spunk? What a wife and mother she was! Young yet brilliant, she grew the International Commodity Co-op into an enterprise that literally kept alive millions around the globe who refused the mark of Antichrist and lost their legal right to buy and sell.

"In various safe-house locations over the past half dozen years, I lived in close proximity to Chloe and to her family. It was common to find her reading her Bible, memorizing verses, trying them out on people. Often she would hand me her Bible and ask me to check her to see if she had a verse correct, word for word. And she always wanted to know exactly what it meant. It was not enough to know the text; she wanted it to come alive in her heart and mind and life.

"To those who will miss Chloe the most, the deepest, and the most painfully until we see her again in glory, I give you the only counsel that kept me sane when my own beloved were so cruelly taken from me. Hold to God's unchanging hand. Cling to his

Word. Fall in love with the Word of God anew. Grasp his promises like a puppy sinks its teeth into your pant legs, and never let go.

"Buck, Kenny, Rayford, we do not understand. We cannot. We are finite beings. The Scripture says knowledge is so fleeting that one day it will vanish. 'For we know in part and we prophesy in part. But when that which is perfect has come,' and oh, beloved, it is coming, 'then that which is in part will be done away.

"'When I was a child, I spoke as a child, I understood as a child, I thought as a child; but when I became a man, I put away childish things. For now we see in a mirror, dimly, but then face to face.'

"Did you hear that promise? 'But then . . .' How we can rejoice in the but thens of God's Word! The then is coming, dear ones! The then is coming."

14. How were Albie and Chloe remembered? What was important to each of them?

_____

_____

_____

_____

_____

_____

15. If your funeral were being held tomorrow and the speakers in the service were completely honest, how would you be remembered?

_____

_____

_____

_____

_____

16. If Christ really is coming again soon (and, of course, he *is!*), how does that fact affect the way you spend your time?

_____

_____

_____

_____

_____

_____

_____

17. What would you say are the three most important reasons for studying the Bible in these last days?

a. _____

_____

_____

b. _____

_____

_____

c. _____

_____

_____

"The second coming of Jesus Christ . . . is what prophecy is primarily about. It is doubtless the greatest story of the future to be found anywhere. No religion, no culture, and no literature offers such a sublime concept of future events that lead into an even better eternity. Once understood, these thrilling events prove so exciting and inspiring that many have turned from their sins to find Christ as their Lord and Savior—good reason for all Christians to know about them, particularly as we see so many of these events fulfilled in our lifetime." [5]

Tim LaHaye and Jerry Jenkins

Making the Change

Read this passage from Isaiah 34:

Come here and listen, O nations of the earth. Let the world and everything in it hear my words. For the LORD is enraged against the nations. His fury is against all their armies. He will completely destroy them, bringing about their slaughter. Their dead will be left *unburied, and the stench of rotting bodies will fill the land. The mountains will flow with their blood. The heavens above will melt away and disappear like a rolled-up scroll. The stars will fall from the sky, just as withered leaves and fruit fall from a tree.*

*And when my sword has finished its work in the heavens, then watch. It will fall upon Edom, the nation I have completely destroyed. The sword of the L*ORD *is drenched with blood. It is covered with fat as though it had been used for killing lambs and goats and rams for a sacrifice. Yes, the L*ORD *will offer a great sacrifice in the rich city of Bozrah. He will make a mighty slaughter in Edom. The strongest will die—veterans and young men, too. The land will be soaked with blood and the soil enriched with fat. For it is the day of the L*ORD's *vengeance, the year when Edom will be paid back for all it did to Israel.* (Isaiah 34:1–8)

18. What indications do you see that this passage connects the Glorious Appearing of Christ with the event called Armageddon?

_____

_____

_____

_____

_____

19. If you are a believer in Jesus, to what degree are you obediently walking with Christ right now? What areas of your life need added attention?

_____

_____

_____

_____

_____

20. What three people in your extended family have you spoken to the least about Christ and the forgiveness, hope, and life he offers? Would you be willing to have an exploratory conversation with one of those people, if God clearly provided the opportunity? (If so, take time to pray for that opportunity.)

_____

_____

"Lift up your eyes and look out on a world that is desperate and discouraged, concerned and confused. . . . Now realize that Christ has no hands but yours to reach out to this world. If you know Jesus Christ as your Savior, then he expects you to be active for him. The time might be short, but use what time he gives you to make an eternal difference in others' lives."[6]

Larry Mercer

Pursuing the Truth

All great stories come full circle. The problem or mystery introduced in the beginning is resolved in the end. Good triumphs over evil. Loose ends get wrapped up. Certainly this is true on the cosmic level with God's story. Pastor and author Tony Evans describes it this way:

> *Christ's return and victory over Satan will be the culmination of the reason for which mankind was created in the first place. This takes us all the way back . . . to the angelic conflict that began in heaven.*
>
> *God created man as a lesser being than the angels to demonstrate his power to Satan and all the angels who followed him in rebellion (Genesis 1:26–28; Psalm 8:3–6). God said to Satan, in effect, 'I am going to defeat you through a man' (Daniel 7:13–14; Hebrews 2:5–8, 14).*
>
> *So Satan went after Adam and Eve, and he figured he had checkmated God when Adam fell. But God promised a coming—another man named Jesus Christ, the Last Adam—through whom God would ultimately triumph. Satan didn't bank on God becoming a man in the person of Christ.*
>
> *Satan went after Christ, too, first at his birth and then on the cross, but to no avail. Now, at Armageddon, we see Jesus and redeemed mankind in the armies of heaven coming to administer Satan's defeat. Jesus Christ is God's agent of judgment as well as his agent of redemption.*[7]

21. Review Tony Evans's outline of the "big story" of the universe above. Then jot down a few sentences, telling in your own words the twists and turns of God's plan.

_____

_____

_____

_____

_____

_____

_____

23. How does Matthew 24:29–31 describe the return of the Lord? How will the watching world respond?

_____

_____

_____

_____

_____

_____

_____

Lesson in Review . . .

- When the enemies of God have amassed at Armageddon at the end of the Tribulation period to destroy the surviving people of God, Christ will return suddenly and dramatically.
- The whole world will see this "Glorious Appearing" of our great God and Savior, Jesus Christ.
- Faithful believers will be thrilled at the return of their King, and receive a reward.
- Unbelievers will experience the severe justice of the One they have rejected.

LEFT

BEHIND

Armageddon

Lesson 6:
The Battle Won!

1. What has been one of the greatest achievements or accomplishments of your life? How did you feel at the moment of success or victory?

_____

_____

_____

_____

_____

2. During what movie did you cheer the loudest when the hero finally "got the bad guy"?

_____

_____

_____

_____

_____

Unfolding the Story
(Armageddon, pp. 230–33)

There is a memorable scene in *Armageddon* that illustrates the ultimate triumph of the Christian faith. Chloe Williams has been captured by the Global Community security forces of Antichrist Nicolae Carpathia. Her prospects for rescue or survival do not look good, and yet she feels a strange, unearthly peace, and an inner certainty that she is on the winning side.

IN PERVASIVE DARKNESS, Chloe had no idea of the passage of time. Occasionally she pressed her ear against the steel door to listen for activity in the solitary unit. So far, nothing.

She thought waiting for one's execution would be like waiting to see the principal or facing a punishment you knew was coming, only multiplied on a mortal scale. And yet she found herself relatively calm. Her heart broke for Buck, not so much for the prospect of his missing her, but for how wrenching it would be to have to explain this to Kenny.

He was too young, and there would be no explaining it, she knew. But the daily questions, the need of a boy for his mother, the fact that no surrogate could love him like she did, . . . all that worked on her.

Chloe felt the presence of God, though she didn't see the messenger she had the night before. Her muscles ached from the positions she found herself in for prayer and then just trying to get comfortable. Hunger was a distraction she succeeded in pushing from her mind. Soon, she told herself, she would be dining at the banquet table of the King of kings.

Most gratifying was that she had fewer doubts and more assurance as the hours passed. She had put all her eggs in this basket, she had always liked to say. If she was wrong, she was wrong. If it was all a big story, she had bought it in its entirety. But for her the days of questioning and misgivings were gone. Chloe had seen too much, experienced too much. She had been shown, like everyone else on the planet, that God was real, he was in control, he was the archenemy of Antichrist, and in the end God would win. . . .

She didn't even know what to do with her feelings of love and concern and sympathy for people who had already taken Carpathia's mark and were condemned for eternity. They were beyond help and hope, and yet still she grieved for them. Flashes of humanity in Florence, in Nigel, in Jesse, in Jock . . . what did those mean? She couldn't expect unbelievers to live like believers, and so she was left without the option to judge them—only to love them. Yet it was hopeless now.

While Chloe couldn't understand how there could still be uncommitted people in the world, she knew there were. Those were the ones she would try to reach with whatever freedom God made the GC give her to make a last comment. How someone could see all that had gone on during the last six years and not realize that the only options were God or Satan—or worse, could know the options and yet choose Satan— she could not fathom.

But no doubt this was true. Ming had told her of Muslims who were anti-Carpathia because they were so devout in their own faith. Some practicing Jews who did not believe in Jesus as Messiah also rejected Carpathia as god of this world. George knew of militia types who refused to give allegiance to a dictator yet had not trusted Christ for their salvation either.

Was it possible, after all this time, that there were still spiritually uncommitted people who simply hadn't chosen yet? Chloe couldn't imagine, but she knew it had to be true. Some simply chose to pursue their own goals, their own lusts.

Chloe wondered about the others in Stateville who would die that morning. Many would be bearers of Carpathia's mark, but surely many would not. Would she, as the prize arrest, be last on the docket?

"Clarity, Lord," she said. "That's all I ask for. You have already promised grace and strength. Just let my mind work better than it should under the circumstances."

3. How would you explain to a skeptic the peace that Chloe felt? How would you illustrate that peace from your own life?

_____

_____

_____

_____

_____

4. According to this excerpt, what might be some of the reasons people will follow neither Christ nor the Antichrist?

_____

_____

_____

_____

5. What motivated Chloe to pray for clarity? Why would that quality be so important?

_____

_____

_____

_____

Back to Reality

A great many books and movies have hard-to-swallow, even ludicrous endings. Heroes surviving massive explosions or horrific wrecks. Bad guys being felled by a one-in-a-trillion lucky shot. Hollywood asks its audience to suspend all logic and to believe impossible things. Not so with the Left Behind books. The goal of the authors is not to dream up some kind of unbelievable fantasy but to convey realistically what the Bible suggests about the final days of earth as we know it.

6. In what ways do you find it challenging to envision a world in which evil truly has been vanquished and Christ is literally reigning?

7. What excites you most about the second coming, the "Glorious Appearing," of Christ?

In Isaiah 46:9–10, God says:

> And do not forget the things I have done throughout history. For I am God—I alone! I am God, and there is no one else like me. Only I can tell you what is going to happen even before it happens. Everything I plan will come to pass, for I do whatever I wish.

8. How does this passage affect your thinking regarding the final victory of Christ?

Understanding the Word

In lesson 5, we looked at the Glorious Appearing of Christ, arriving from heaven just in the nick of time, to save his people and destroy his enemies. We looked carefully at his appearance and we experienced the awe and triumph of his sovereign power.

Here we want to see the inevitable consequences of the coming of earth's ultimate King, Judge, and Lord. Consider this passage from the great Hebrew prophet Zechariah:

Watch, for the day of the LORD is coming when your possessions will be plundered right in front of you! On that day I will gather all the nations to fight against Jerusalem. The city will be taken, the houses plundered, and the women raped. Half the population will be taken away into captivity, and half will be left among the ruins of the city.

Then the LORD will go out to fight against those nations, as he has fought in times past. On that day his feet will stand on the Mount of Olives, which faces Jerusalem on the east. And the Mount of Olives will split apart, making a wide valley running from east to west, for half the mountain will move toward the north and half toward the south. You will flee through this valley, for it will reach across to Azal. Yes, you will flee as you did from the earthquake in the days of King Uzziah of Judah. Then the LORD *my God will come, and all his holy ones with him.*

On that day the sources of light will no longer shine, yet there will be continuous day! Only the LORD *knows how this could happen! There will be no normal day and night, for at evening time it will still be light. On that day life-giving waters will flow out from Jerusalem, half toward the Dead Sea and half toward the Mediterranean, flowing continuously both in summer and in winter.*

And the LORD *will be king over all the earth. On that day there will be one* LORD—*his name alone will be worshiped. All the land from Geba, north of Judah, to Rimmon, south of Jerusalem, will become one vast plain. But Jerusalem will be raised up in its original place and will be inhabited all the way from the Benjamin Gate over to the site of the old gate, then to the Corner Gate, and from the Tower of Hananel to the king's winepresses. And Jerusalem will be filled, safe at last, never again to be cursed and destroyed.*

And the LORD *will send a plague on all the nations that fought against Jerusalem. Their people will become like walking corpses, their flesh rotting away. Their eyes will shrivel in their sockets, and their tongues will decay in their mouths. On that day they will be terrified, stricken by the* LORD *with great panic. They will fight against each other in hand-to-hand combat; Judah, too, will be fighting at Jerusalem. The wealth of all the neighboring nations will be captured—great quantities of gold and silver and fine clothing. This same plague will strike the horses, mules, camels, donkeys, and all the other animals in the enemy camps.* (Zechariah 14:1–14)

9. According to these verses, what will happen to Jerusalem at the time of Armageddon (verse 2)?

_____

_____

_____

_____

10. How will the Lord defend his people? Where will he make his victorious ascent (verse 4)?

_____

_____

_____

_____

11. What supernatural phenomena unfolds as the Lord takes complete control of the world?

_____

_____

_____

_____

_____

Now read these prophetic words of Joel:

> "Now let the sickle do its work, for the harvest is ripe. Come, tread the winepress because it is full. The storage vats are overflowing with the wickedness of these people."
>
> Thousands upon thousands are waiting in the valley of decision. It is there that the day of the LORD will soon arrive. The sun and moon will grow dark, and the stars will no longer shine. The LORD's voice will roar from Zion and thunder from Jerusalem, and the earth and heavens will begin to shake. But to his people of Israel, the LORD will be a welcoming refuge and a strong fortress.
>
> "Then you will know that I, the LORD your God, live in Zion, my holy mountain. Jerusalem will be holy forever, and foreign armies will never conquer her again. (Joel 3:13–17)

12. What does this passage add to your understanding of Christ's second advent victory over the enemies of God?

_____

_____

_____

_____

_____

"On the great day of his return, Christ will defeat all his enemies, capture alive the Antichrist and the false prophet, and cast them into the lake of fire, where they will be tormented day and night forever and ever (Revelation 20:1–3). The birds of the air and the beasts of the field will feast on the corpses of the slain, and no one who resists Christ will remain alive." [2]

Tim LaHaye and Jerry Jenkins

Finding the Connection

In a world that feels very much out of control, one of the greatest testimonies Christians can present of the reality and power of God is a life filled with peace.

When we trust that God is in control, when we put our confidence in the promises and truths that are the focus of these Left Behind study guides, when we refuse to listen to the damnable lies of the Evil One, when we resist the temptation to panic in the face of crisis, . . . THEN the world sees something alluring and attractive in us.

This peace that surpasses all human understanding—God's peace—is a precious, priceless gift. In the words of the old campfire song, "The world didn't give it, and the world can't take it away."

13. Describe in a few phrases the quality of peace that you have in your soul.

_____

_____

_____

_____

14. What would you tell a restless, anxious friend about how to find true, lasting peace of soul?

_____

_____

_____

_____

15. Consider 2 Kings 19:35 as an unusual reason for peace in the midst of apparent difficulties. How many invading soldiers were killed in one night by the power of the angel of the Lord? What does this suggest about the Lord's power to instantly decimate the forces of the world's nations at Armageddon?

_____

_____

_____

_____

> "In a sense, Armageddon is a battle that never really takes place. That is, it does not take place in accordance with its original human intent. Its human purpose is to gather the armies of the world to execute the Antichrist's final solution to the 'Jewish problem.' This is why Jesus Christ chooses this moment in history for his return to Earth—to thwart the Antichrist's attempted annihilation of the Jews and to destroy the armies of the world, which were gathered for another purpose. It seems only fitting, in light of mankind's bloody legacy, that the return of Christ should be precipitated by a worldwide military conflict against Israel. So it is that history is moving toward Armageddon." [3]
>
> Tim LaHaye and Thomas Ice

Making the Change

(Armageddon, pp. 369–70)

To call the gospel of Jesus Christ "good news" is, in one sense, the understatement of the ages. In fact, the message of Jesus is the best and greatest of all possible news. The gospel proclaims that God is, that he inexplicably loves this old dying world, that he sent his Son Jesus to rescue us, that Christ died willingly to pay for our foolish sins, that our Savior rose from the dead, that Jesus will return and reign forever. The gospel further assures us that we will be with our Creator and Sustainer and King for all eternity.

The more we ponder the implications of our faith, the more we are filled to overflowing with hope and joy, like Buck Williams in this scene from *Armageddon:*

"RABBI! TEACH US some more."

Buck looked to Tsion, who shrugged. "That is why I came. If they want to listen, I want to preach."

As soon as he began, curious crowds gathered again. And as Buck watched and listened, he was overcome with the privilege of being where he was and when it was. He sensed he could see Jesus at any time. And Chloe.

To hear God's man in God's place at God's time—what an unspeakable privilege. Scared? Of course he was. Wondering if Jesus would really come when he said he would? Not even a question. Buck couldn't wait. He just couldn't wait.

16. How excited are you—really—at the prospect of the Lord's imminent return? How would someone else spot that excitement in your life?

_____

_____

_____

_____

_____

_____

17. Given the Lord's total and certain victory over the Evil One, why do so many Christians live with fear and uncertainty?

_____

_____

_____

_____

_____

_____

18. As you approach the end of this study, knowing a little better what the Bible assures us regarding the future, how should believers live in the end times?

_____

_____

_____

_____

_____

19. If you've read any books about D-Day or seen movies about that great assault at Normandy, you know that almost all the soldiers who just hunkered down on the beach ended up dead or wounded. Ironically, most of the soldiers who avoided serious injury were the ones who kept fighting and moving forward. How could that principle be used as an analogy about spiritual warfare in these last days?

_____

_____

_____

_____

_____

> "From the time of the very earliest civilizations, our world has known conflict and wars. There has never been an extended period of true peace at any one time all over the globe. Even during the times when weapons have been set aside, there has been verbal, emotional, and political discord and hatred between people groups. Man, with his sin nature, is simply not capable of bringing true and lasting peace to the world.
>
> "Only when the Prince of Peace, Jesus Christ, comes to the world and sets up his kingdom will there be real harmony and peace. He is the only one who has the power and ability to enforce the peace, righteousness, and abundance that will mark the thousand-year earthly utopia known as the millennial kingdom." [4]
>
> Tim LaHaye and Thomas Ice

Pursuing the Truth

20. Isaiah 65:19–25 gives us a description of Christ's coming kingdom. What strikes you as most intriguing or exciting about this description?

_____

_____

_____

_____

_____

21. Revelation 1:3 says: "God blesses the one who reads this prophecy to the church, and he blesses all who listen to it and obey what it says. For the time is near when these things will happen." How does this promise challenge you today?

_____

_____

_____

_____

22. In what specific ways is God urging you or nudging you toward listening and obeying as a result of this study? What do you need to begin doing—or stop doing?

_____

_____

_____

_____

_____

"Friends, he is coming again, and he will do so quickly! Are you ready? John was, so he could write [in the book of Revelation] with gladness, 'And the Spirit and the bride say, "Come!" And let him who hears say, "Come!"' (22:17). But he wasn't content to leave it at that. He knew some might be reading his book who weren't ready for the Lord's return. So to them he writes, 'And let him who thirsts come. And whoever desires, let him take the water of life freely' (22:17).

"Are you thirsty? Then come to Christ, so that you will be ready when he comes. Do you desire to quench your thirst at the great fountain of God? Then come and take that water freely. Drink deeply of his cool, refreshing waters. Cast yourself wholly upon his grace, and ask Jesus to satisfy your soul. Then you, too, will be ready to say with John, 'Even so, come, Lord Jesus!'" [5]

Tim LaHaye and Jerry Jenkins

Lesson in Review . . .

- The second coming of Christ will result in the crushing defeat of Satan and the enemies of God at Armageddon.
- Following his military victory and the judgment of his foes, Christ will begin to rule the earth in perfect justice. His kingdom will be a kind of "heaven on earth."
- Christians can look forward to the future with confidence and joy—knowing that we serve an all-powerful King and Lord before whom every knee will bow. History really is "his story"!

Endnotes

Lesson 1: To End All Wars

1. Tim LaHaye and Thomas Ice, *Charting the End Times* (Eugene, Ore.: Harvest House, 2001), 65.
2. John F. Walvoord, *End Times: Understanding Today's World Events in Biblical Prophecy* (Nashville: Word, 1998), 221.
3. Tony Evans, *The Best Is Yet to Come* (Chicago: Moody, 2000), 199.
4. Ibid., 202.
5. LaHaye and Ice, *Charting the End Times*, 63.
6. Evans, *The Best Is Yet to Come*, 213.

Lesson 2: The Gathering Storm

1. Tim LaHaye and Thomas Ice, *Charting the End Times* (Eugene, Ore.: Harvest House, 2001), 62.
2. John F. Walvoord, *The Prophecy Knowledge Handbook* (Wheaton: Victor, 1990), 612.
3. Tim LaHaye and Jerry B. Jenkins, *Are We Living in the End Times?* (Wheaton: Tyndale House, 1999), 36–37.
4. Charles C. Ryrie, *The Ryrie Study Bible* (Chicago: Moody, 1978), 1284.
5. LaHaye and Ice, *Charting the End Times*, 70.

Lesson 3: "In This Corner . . ."

1. John F. Walvoord, *Armageddon, Oil, and the Middle East Crisis* (Grand Rapids: Zondervan, 1974), 164–65.
2. Tim LaHaye and Jerry Jenkins, *Are We Living in the End Times?* (Wheaton: Tyndale House, 1999), 209–10.
3. Tim LaHaye and Thomas Ice, *Charting the End Times* (Eugene, Ore.: Harvest House, 2001), 93.
4. Samuel Naaman, "The Future of Islamic Fundamentalism," in *Prophecy in Light of Today,* ed. Charles Dyer (Chicago: Moody, 2002), 66–68.

Lesson 4: Surrounded!

1. Tim LaHaye and Thomas Ice, *Charting the End Times* (Eugene, Ore.: Harvest House, 2001), 68.

2. John F. Walvoord, *End Times: Understanding Today's World Events in Biblical Prophecy* (Nashville: Word, 1998), 1–2.

3. Ibid., 3.

4. Tony Evans, *The Best Is Yet to Come* (Chicago: Moody, 2000), 20–21.

5. LaHaye and Ice, *Charting the End Times,* 68.

Lesson 5: The Arrival of the King

1. Tim LaHaye and Jerry Jenkins, *Are We Living in the End Times?* (Wheaton: Tyndale House, 1999), 221–22.

2. John F. Walvoord, *Armageddon, Oil, and the Middle East Crisis* (Grand Rapids: Zondervan, 1974), 169.

3. LaHaye and Jenkins, *Are We Living in the End Times?* 228.

4. Tony Evans, *The Best Is Yet to Come* (Chicago: Moody, 2000), 219.

5. LaHaye and Jenkins, *Are We Living in the End Times?* 8.

6. Larry Mercer, "How Should We Then Live?" in *Prophecy in Light of Today,* ed. Charles Dyer (Chicago: Moody, 2002), 126–27.

7. Evans, *The Best Is Yet to Come,* 215.

Lesson 6: The Battle Won!

1. Tim LaHaye and Jerry Jenkins, *Are We Living in the End Times?* (Wheaton: Tyndale House, 1999), 228–29.

2. Ibid., 229.

3. Tim LaHaye and Thomas Ice, *Charting the End Times* (Eugene, Ore.: Harvest House, 2001), 63.

4. Ibid., 78.

5. LaHaye and Jenkins, *Are We Living in the End Times?* 232.